Everyday Excellence

The Art of Success

Sadhana Singh

Kundalini Research Institute

Training ❧ Publishing ❧ Research ❧ Resources

Published by the Kundalini Research Institute

PO Box 1819
Santa Cruz, NM 87532
www.kundaliniresearchinstitute.org
ISBN 978-1-934532-85-0

Editor: Sat Purkh Kaur Khalsa
KRI Review: Siri Neel Kaur Khalsa
Consulting Editor: Nirvair Singh Khalsa
Copy Editor: Tara Joffe
Design and Layout: Prana Projects: Ditta Khalsa, Biljana Nedelkovska
Photography: Alessandro Valeri
Model: Hari Rai Kaur
Back cover portrait of Sadhana Singh by Coco Van Oppens

My thanks goes to Hari Bhajan Kaur for her revision of the first draft. And I cannot say enough about the dedication of Uttamjit Kaur, who revised the second draft, translated the text, and worked with the publisher, author and editor to bring this project to fruition. Thank you and many blessings, Sadhana Singh..

The purpose of all branches of yoga
is to raise the Kundalini,
to raise the dormant power of the being
so that one can have excellence.[1]

⁓Yogi Bhajan

Table of Contents

Introduction

Excellence is discovering who we are and having the courage to manifest it. To excel is to be out of the ordinary—extraordinary. It is possible for each of us to achieve excellence, because it is a basic skill inherent in every human being. Excellence is a constant attitude of rising above the pressures and constraints of time and space, so that the mind may tune into the soul's frequency.

Instinctively and inevitably we relate to things, to people, and to ourselves in superficial ways, and often we understand and experience only that which our mind and our belief systems are willing to support. Until we reach excellence, ours is a tendency to survive, more than thrive. The mind, by itself, is not able to be in touch with reality, to have a true contact with reality: Any input we give the mind, the mind sees as reality. The mind cannot compute what is true and what is not; it needs to be guided by our consciousness. Our mind can sometimes work against us, to the detriment of our essence and identity. If the mind isn't consciously directed by us, its constant activity of producing and processing thoughts and feelings inevitably leads to failure and to the patterns that contribute to failure again and again. Life needs our involvement, and our mind needs to be under conscious supervision so that we are directed toward reality. Discipline is the medium that helps us relate consciously to the mind so that it serves our essence and our purpose.

Life offers an extraordinary opportunity for each of us to excel, and there are many different techniques, approaches, and lifestyles to support our evolutionary process. This book explores the ancient system of Kundalini Yoga and Yogi Bhajan's teachings on excellence. This is my humble attempt to share Yogi Bhajan's Eight Elements of Excellence and how they have supported and guided me, from the very beginning of my journey, toward grasping this precious opportunity to excel as a human being.

We are often not aware of who we really are, what impact our presence has, and how we influence space and time. It's only when we look back on our lives that we become aware that every thing, person, or situation that we encountered was attracted to us by us. Our environments, along with the people in our lives, influence us just as much as we influence them. Everything we experience has been filtered by our minds. We have the innate ability to co-create reality—to both influence and be influenced. Why not direct this potential consciously and clearly?

That which our mind believes possible is the only reality feasible for us. The mind operates from an inherent polarity—yes or no, black or white, fear or love—and this game of polarity wins the mind's attention. Those two possibilities become the only things that, in our perception, can happen, but they are nothing more than an infinitesimal slice of the infinite range of possibilities available. Be it a subconscious fear, a conscious fantasy, a threatening idea, or a burst of inspiration, the mind attaches to a thought, after having colored that thought and changed its original essence based on the mind's belief patterns. This then becomes the reality that the mind believes in. Therefore, discipline of the mind is essential; otherwise we will be more dependent on hope than on intention or action. Yet hope weighs little against the gravity of our own, stronger fears.

Life has taught me that when you really want something, you have to want it inside and out for it to manifest perfectly. Deep intention and outward projection must be accomplices in this game called life. For years, I would energetically weave the conditions in order to make something happen that I wanted; I would dedicate time and energy to it, and yet my thoughts were filled with duality: "Will it, or will it not? Will I be able to grasp the opportunity? Will I be successful? And once successful, will I be able to sustain success? And once satisfied, how will I maintain that satisfaction?" This kind of thinking would always accompany me, be it in love, sports, or work. When I look back on those times, I wonder how much I really wanted to succeed, on what basis I had made my choices, and whether I was consistent with myself or whether I only wanted to prove something or simply needed to cover bigger emotional or existential gaps in my life.

With the help of yoga, I now understand the mechanisms of the mind and see its dynamics at play. Every intention stems from personality, emotion, and duality. If we don't have a solid understanding of ourselves, we end up living, striving, and suffering for something that has nothing to do with who we are and that does not serve our true purpose or mission. We live someone else's life, pretending to be happy. It's like waking up one morning and feeling like a tired, wounded warrior who realizes he was fighting the wrong battle. Most of the time, a hypocritical game is being played beneath our desires: We keep saying we want something that, inwardly, we know we do not want. So, of course, that something keeps not happening, thus granting us permission to continue complaining and feeling like victims—we are simply seeking to feel that stinging sense of something missing. Yoga, however, gradually leads us to recognize who we are and helps us decide how to improve, grow, and change so that we can expand and manifest on multiple levels. In my own life, the first part—recognizing who I am—led me to meet my Master. The second part—improving, growing, and changing—is still expanding as I apply the teachings.

Once in us, Yogi Bhajan's Eight Elements of Excellence form an amalgam that makes us cohesive, clear, and effective. Far from being a strategy, the Eight Elements are the qualities and attitudes, the anatomy and physiology, of an organic unity that vibrates the attitude to excel within every cell. To excel means to go beyond, out of the cell, trespassing beyond given limits and boundaries, to rise, to project. Through adventure after adventure, we move away from what is known and familiar to the unknown, so that the unknown may become known. When our physical, psychological, and energetic parameters tell us it is impossible to move forward and progress, we have arrived at the cell membrane of who we know ourselves to be. But when we start to go beyond that border, excellence begins. We all try to reinforce our current position with knowledge and skills, prejudice and fear, but it doesn't work: Life becomes flat, painful, sometimes even comfortably painful and briefly pleasant. What many of us have not tried is understanding who we are, accepting ourselves, and then finding the strength to go beyond our self-imposed limits.

In this book, we will find out about leaving the known cellular environment—where things either make sense or they don't, where things seem possible or impossible—and entering a state of awareness in which we learn that life is nothing more than making sense of something that has no sense. We then meet or create another non-sense and transform it again and again, up and down like the tides. This is the spice of life, and these are the catalysts of excellence.

The first rule of any business, challenge, relationship, or game is knowing the playing field and the rules. The playground where we train the muscle of awareness is life, an experience in time and space during which we apply the art of relating to ourselves and to others. By studying the polarities within our own lives, we learn to apply our experiences in order to progress and excel. This playground is like a network of energy lines, and these lines are the warp and woof of the fabric that makes up the universe where we live. In Kundalini Yoga, this network is called tantra, and it is held together by polarity. These points of polarity make up the web on which we weave our life.

Polarities are like the cushions of a pool table: The ball crashes into the cushion, bounces off in a different direction, and rolls into the hole you were aiming for. Like in a game of pool, with its rules given by polarity, dharma (the wise and righteous path) is the process that traces the most direct line between you and your destiny. Even applying the Eight Elements of Excellence, we have to face the suffering that comes with polarity, but if we're in the game at all, we come out winners.

In Kundalini Yoga, life is the study of comparative polarity. In order to know it, we have to relate to it. But we'll never be able to really relate to the nature of polarity until we understand that it must not be fought, judged, or resolved; it must simply be accepted. In order to grow in awareness, we must gradually leave behind the concepts of right and wrong. Our sense of right and wrong often accompanies—if it's not purely derived from—what we want. Our own desires serve to block or limit the experience of the moment. When we continually label something as right or wrong, we remove ourselves from the experience at hand. The intensity and depth of what we feel when we are present to that experience—in the precise moment, as it happens—are both wonderful and terrible at the same time. Regardless of the content of the experience, which can cause joy or sadness, boredom or excitement, being present to it is often overwhelming. So we resist it, fight it, describe it, comment on it, judge it—but all of these reactions are equal to losing the experience altogether.

We can revive the experience in our memory to understand it, but it becomes a distortion that has been reworked through our thought patterns and preconceptions. Recounting it to ourselves or to others will only make us lose its truth. To live is to be in the experience of what happens—in the fundamental here and now. Any alternative is just an existential journey in which we escape, avoid, or replace ourselves. Each time we allow ourselves to be totally in the experience of the relationship that we are living (be it a relationship to an object, a situation, a thought, or a person)—when we allow ourselves to be guided by awareness, without reacting—we expand beyond our assumed or imaginary limits, giving rise to our own excellence. In this way, any challenge, disaster, or circumstance can be perceived as a possibility, in that it offers a possibility to excel.

From where we relate to something or someone is crucial. In order to relate, we have to do it from our true self and not be influenced by prejudice. To grasp the true self, we need to find our inner silence; we must stop the flow of thoughts and establish a relationship from the heart of the mind and from the mind of the heart. If the relationship dwells within these parameters, then it is truth.

The faculty of being in silence is already excellence, because we are in a conscious and intuitive space, beyond the limits of intellect and reason. From this state, any barrier to excellence will fall into decay, and the range of the infinite possibilities will exist in proportion to what we allow ourselves to experience. These steps in consciousness rarely take place in an automatic or natural way. In fact, there is a trend that keeps us in a restricted and defensive hypnotic state. We call this state mediocrity, which is the polar opposite of excellence.

Whoever has achieved happiness has first gone through hell. Whoever feels free has been disciplined. Whoever has been successful has made the decision to become successful. Decision-making, free will, and willpower are key factors in excelling. To apply ourselves, stretch out, and discipline ourselves is not enough. We must be prepared to sacrifice the safety of what we know, our own limitations, and we must want to excel. These few basic concepts can be found in a sentence of Yogi Bhajan that only recently revealed itself to me:

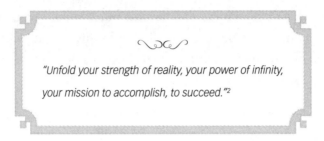

"Unfold your strength of reality, your power of infinity, your mission to accomplish, to succeed."[2]

The strength of your own reality is created by who you are and by your ability to relate neutrally to truth. Once you have found yourself, your first relationship is with the Infinite—that same infinite power that lives in you. Accepting who you are and your role within the Infinite gives you presence. If, according to your will, your presence marries your role and strives to make it your mission, then the path to your destiny will be manifest. To follow that path, you have to exceed beyond your own illusory limits and imaginary disabilities. Whether you try, succeed, or die trying, that is excellence.

In the past, my inability to stay in the depths of a relationship was the anchor that kept me in mediocrity. Situations and people remained suspended as memories, each one tied to special feelings that colored my inner world. The cage in which I lived made me experience a comfortable range of moods, a stagnant feeling of oppressed security. It made me feel protected, but not happy. It wasn't exciting, but it was recognizable and acceptable. Today my memories of that time offer a rich landscape that encourages me to do better, to stay in the depths, not to give in, so that my relationships grow exponentially and are uplifting to all parties. To better understand this idea, let's move our attention to observe the "true self" in others in order to comprehend the impact they have on us and on how we can stay in relationship with them.

Sometimes, in relation to the women in my life, I would feel love—or rediscovered love—when they opened up, allowing a beauty and light to shine through that could only be ascribable to their souls. A window would open that made them unique, unforgettable, beautiful, and superior. In that moment—when they were their own selves, open and true—a connection was created between us that, from that moment onward, would always confirm a feeling of full and constant love, beyond life's circumstances. When a relationship happens with such intensity that the two polarities—or people—meet in the glory and perfection of their true selves, that relationship becomes authentic. The problem is having the courage to keep that intensity, with all the risks and wonders doing so brings. If we cannot sustain the relationship's intensity, we may end up spending fifty years confronting each other's personality, sharing and struggling, maybe even achieving intimacy, confidence, and knowledge with each other—but not love. If we are not completely ourselves, we cannot fully experience the depth of give-and-take required by a relationship. We simply become connoisseurs of each other's weaknesses, games, mental intrigues, and defenses, rather than true lovers. We sometimes say we loved someone as if the concept of love could be reduced to an action in the past, when in reality, love knows only the simple present.

What does love have to do with excellence? Everything. Love is the creative, expansive energy of the universe. If you can bring love into everything you do, then you will excel. Allowing ourselves to imagine that love is possible—not only toward beauty or a lover, but also toward an idea, a project, our own life or somebody else's, a common cause, a service—may help us begin to get a clue of where excellence can lead us.

When we take into consideration the pressures and constraints that invade our lives right now, everything we have talked about until now, even if it sounds great, may seem pure philosophy. From where we stand, we can think, plan, change the order of things, or hide them, but there is no solution, let alone evolution, to the problem. Instead we need to change gears and shift into a new consciousness so that what was once a problem or difficulty may now be perceived as an opportunity, so that the impossible may become possible. The aim is to break through our own comfort level, while keeping a strong core, a strong sense of self. To do this we need two things—posture and attitude—nothing more. Posture is a common point where deep intention and external projection meet, and attitude is a predisposition of the soul to act. Both reinforce each other and interact with one another to remind us of who we want to be, and then they communicate that to the universe.

From the core of ourselves, we expand beyond our limits, projecting our vibrational frequency. The universe responds because we can influence our own environment and attract favorable circumstances that will serve our purpose. This is the concept of "desire to deserve," which says we must create the conditions, the chemistry, the energy structures, and the synergy that help us believe it is possible to excel. Only then can we convince all of creation of this possibility so that the universe will come to serve us. Life responds to who we think we are and who we project ourselves to be. Thus, if we do not believe in ourselves, how can we expect someone else to believe in us? The Eight Elements of Excellence give us the appropriate posture and attitude to create glandular maturity, strength of the nervous system, and abundance of neural maps, so that our very presence, our smell, and our radiance may express excellence, without us having to say a word.

A student once asked his teacher, "How can I get rid of all my problems?" The teacher replied, "Go under a tree, sit down, and smile." The student, probably desperate enough to obey, went under a tree, sat down, and smiled. After a couple of days, he started getting hungry, but still he sat and smiled. On the fourth day, people began bringing him food. After a month, the flow of people who visited him and appraised him was constant. After six months, people were coming from all over just to see him and feel his presence. It's practical wisdom: to be and to smile, "to be, to be."

What have you done in recent months? Where have you been hiding? What excuses have you made not to come out? Are you weighted down by feelings of guilt or a sense of bad luck? Let's stop playing the usual games. Let's quit going through the maze of mental intrigues. Let's hold our own hand with love and begin to consciously explore the Eight Elements of Excellence.

The following kriya, Unfold the Values and Deliver Success, prepares the ground for each of the meditations that accompany the Eight Elements of Success. Practice it before you initiate the meditation in each chapter and give yourself the chance to truly excel.

Before you begin any practice, always tune in with Ong Namo Guroo Dayv Namo, which means, I bow to the Infinite, I bow to the teacher within.

Kriya to Unfold the Virtues and Deliver Success [3]

January 1, 1981

1. Vayu Manthna Kriya: Sit in Easy Pose and interlace the hands in Venus Lock behind the back, raising the arms as high as possible behind you. Begin twisting, using a powerful breath, building momentum. This exercise is regenerating, making you young and beautiful. It takes care of the complexion, and banishes negativity. Continue for **2-3 minutes**.

2. Immediately place the hands inside the armpits, with elbows out to the sides. The hands will naturally make a fist. Inhale and lift the elbows, exhale and bring them down to the sides, very fast, like wings. The breath will be like a steam engine. Continue for **2-3 minutes**.

3. Extend the arms straight out to the sides, with palms face down, and begin flapping the arms like wings, up and down within 60 degrees. Do not bend the elbows. Inhale up and exhale down through an open mouth. Go faster and faster for **1-2 minutes**. Inhale deeply, exhale and immediately proceed to the next exercise.

4. Lie flat on the back and place the hands, palm down, beneath the lower back. Keep the legs straight and alternately raise them to 90 degrees with Breath of Fire. Pace: Allow 2-3 breaths for the legs to go up and down. Continue **3-4 minutes**. Then inhale deeply, stretching both legs straight up to 90 degrees and hold for 5 seconds. Exhale. Inhale deeply, and relax down.

5. Remaining on the back, clasp the hands in Venus Lock behind the neck, inhale and raise both legs up to 90 degrees, heels together. Exhale and lower them to the floor. Continue for **2–3 minutes**. Immediately proceed to the next exercise.

6. Remain in the same position with the legs together and the hands clasped behind the neck. As the legs raise to 90 degrees, lift the upper body to form a "U" shape. Inhale up, and exhale down, Continue for **2 minutes.** To end: Inhale deeply and quickly come into Easy Pose.

7. Cross the hands over Heart Center. Concentrate all your energy into it as you chant, in a monotone:

**Ardaas Bhaee
Amar Daas Guroo
Amar Daas Guroo
Ardaas Bhaee.**

**Raam Daas Guroo
Raam Daas Guroo
Raam Daas Guroo
Sachee Sahee.**

Continue for **10 minutes**. Then inhale deeply and continue to exercise 8.

8. Archer Pose (one side): Plant the left leg in front and extend the right leg behind you. The left arm is extended out in front, parallel to the floor, as if holding a bow. Pull the right arm back, bending the elbow, so that the right hand is near the armpit. A stretch should be felt across the chest. Eyes are open, focus beyond the left hand, into infinity. Chant aloud for 8 minutes:

Gobinday, Mukanday
Udaaray, Apaaray
Hareeang, Kareeang
Neernaamay, Akaamay

9. Stand with the feet together, extend both arms straight out in front, making a cup with the hands. Stretch the arms out from the shoulder and chant for **4 minutes**. Then Relax.

Aad Sach, Jugaad Sach, Haibhai Sach, Naanak Hosee Bhai Sach.

Chapter One

The Vision

To See Your Goal and Keep It in Your Consciousness

Throughout life, each of us has more visions than we can ever be aware of. We often blur many of those visions in an attempt to understand them from a rational point of view. And yet rarely is a vision vividly clear and immediately meaningful. Instead it's often expressed in the form of a sensation, a déjà vu, an idea, a thought, an image, a word, an internal motion, a particular tendency. As veiled and unpredictable as they may be, however, the methods and timings of a vision are numerous, and our sensory system has an infinite number of ways to perceive of possibilities—those things that are yet to be, the latent potential of things. A vision needs to be coded, similar to how we gather information from a mime, who communicates without words. The mime knows something we don't and finds a way to communicate it. So, too, a part of us extends beyond space and time, draws a vision from the unknown, and translates it to another part of us, using a common language so that the meaning can be grasped and understood by our rational side. Thus, there is a personal interpretation of the vision that depends on how we encode tangible reality. What we perceive and what we see are both filtered by our paradigms and by our habitual ways of interpreting events.

The vision of how we can expand and evolve a possible future may also be achieved through careful assessment of the facts and circumstances, the pros and cons. By analyzing our possibilities and limitations, we can use assessments and pure intellect to develop a strategy and foresee a possible response. Although this rational vision, just like the perceptive vision, is conditioned by our own patterns, it lacks the striking element—that is, the unknown. It does not draw from a new and unpredictable scenario; rather, it draws from the intellect itself. The environment, people, facts, and dynamics are already known and existing. It's like moving furniture around in the same house: As creative as we can be, the result, though good, will always be a displacement of the same elements in the same space.

If we follow the rational process described above, we are analysts reaching a conclusion. If, instead, we follow the perceptive vision, we are visionaries. In the former case, we move on familiar ground; in the latter, there is no ground. One is evolutionary; the other is revolutionary. The vision we want to work from is the perceptive vision, to which we apply our intelligence in order to produce an effective and concrete strategy for manifesting that glimpsed opportunity. Between the vision and its realization is an ocean that must be crossed using the other seven Elements of Excellence.

How many times have you had a vision that made you say, "Now it is clear to me who I am. Now I know where I will go and what I will become"? What did you do with that vision? For most of us, as the reality of the facts remind us of what is possible for us to be and to have, we come to believe our visions less and less, until we see them as pure fantasy. Often, out of laziness, fear, or feelings of guilt and inadequacy, we accept the uncomfortably comfortable situation so as not to risk dealing with a new one. Other times we don't feel the analytical mind's necessary support to determine a strategy, and we aren't able to maintain a continuous and committed state of consciousness. Sometimes we move through the analytical process while remaining attached to the thoughts and visions that haunt us; we try to solve our problems and our discomfort by using the thought itself. As soon as a thought arrives, we experience a momentary relief; we let it take us out of our uncomfortable situation, absolutely unaware of the consequences. Sometimes we escape out of pure impulse—we don't even think about it, we just do it. Why? Because we lack a perceptive vision.

In my early years, before I had begun studying Kundalini Yoga, the paradigm had already begun to take shape, and the vision was starting to blur. Gradually, a veil of preconceptions and memories began to separate me from myself and from the ability to perceive my own life. What must happen to us to reawaken ourselves, for us to rediscover our potential and regain consciousness of our vision to live it and realize it? There must be an opening, a crack in the paradigm, a short circuit in the usual neural pathways, an extraordinary event, a shock, an accident, a revelation. We expect this to happen, hoping to be able to recognize it when it does. But what if instead we trained ourselves every day to make our own paradigm flexible, to reduce the flow of our own thoughts, to create spaces of complete silence from which we can resume the relationship with ourselves and with reality in a new, clear, real way? This is the path of yoga, the noble path that passes through mental silence, or shuniya. Once we reach this stage, we can be sure that our vision is pure and that the relationships we will take from that space will be real.

In a transitional period of my life, before I started practicing Kundalini Yoga, I took up rock climbing. Moving vertically offers a wide range of experiences for understanding yourself and your approach to life. To climb safely, there must be two people: one climbs, and the other acts as security, with equipment that comprises ropes, harnesses, and slings. The safety you receive from the other person is the most important element in climbing, because it offers you the possibility to make mistakes without falling to the ground. It's easy to see how climbing with the thought of falling can be devastating, but to gain confidence in your climbing partner, you have to fall and be saved. The more this happens, the more you can overcome your fear of falling. Likewise, the freedom of action and the relaxed attitude with which you climb, accessing the creative and intuitive physical faculties, are in proportion to how much you trust the other person and the quality of the equipment you're using. The trust you place in your climbing partner on a psychological and relational level reveals the trust you place in the unknown. The unknown is the Infinite, the ultimate partner who will always be with you in any endeavor you want to accomplish in life.

Visual perspectives change radically as you climb up the rock. Flattened against the rock wall, like a lizard, you look up in search of handholds and supports that, in proportion to the difficulty of the selected wall, get smaller and more improbable—sometimes they are only flares or ridges in the rock. From this perspective, what you see is a flat wall; but if you manage to get a little distance, even if only by a few degrees, you could have a better viewing angle, enough to see one or two possibilities. When you are attached to the rock and afraid of the unknown, you're inside the paradigm, and you can't see anything; but when you take a risk and surrender to trust, you break the pattern of thoughts that kept you stuck to your habitual pattern. The same is true in life: If you have trust and you proceed in rising upward, you will have a whole new scenario—new possibilities will reveal themselves to you, creativity will flow, and vision will manifest.

When I took up climbing, the safety I felt, plus the limited vision of my position against the rock wall, laid bare before me the exact awareness of the moment I was in. I could understand the reasons behind my past decisions and life changes. I had been living very impulsively, with a destructive attitude not only toward anything I was able to build, but also toward my successes. Many of my decisions had been dictated by fear, and I don't think I was a very good analyst. I had made my way forward by groping attempts. With an impulsive attitude, based on the two tracks of repulsion and attraction, I went or stayed, fled or fought. But what never ceases to amaze me is that the vision of destiny often unfolded along the very journey I had undertaken in order to avoid it.

A constant sense of incompleteness and dissatisfaction had accompanied the first part of my life: an early childhood, during which I was so calm and slow that my family worried about my delay in walking and talking; an adolescence made of crises and revolt; and finally a coming of age in which I wanted to jump all the stages early. Not happy, I sought satisfaction by doing multiple jobs simultaneously, until I came into the world of fashion, which then led me into the world of acting. In my early twenties, I found myself with a family of my own and work responsibilities—and the consequences that both imply.

Although I was still unhappy, I was fascinated and curious about a world in which my inner drama could be used as an engine in my work. So I began to seriously study acting. I chose Stanislavski's system, a method used to train actors to draw believable emotions into their performances. This method requires profound work on oneself and holds the belief that an actor can capture the essence and nuances of the character he has to play directly from himself. Through a deep understanding of himself, the actor manages to evoke the more remote frequencies of his feelings, to the point of becoming true in his fiction. The sincere and determined application of this method can lead an actor to blossom as a complete human being, able to play any role and, more important, able to come out of it.

Most of our work with the Stanislavski system consisted of relaxation techniques and opening the senses to be able to contact dormant aspects of ourselves, including memories, fears, fantasies, and belief systems. The warm-up stage could last for hours, and only after that would we begin to practice specific exercises, to analyze characters, to improvise. The teachers leading this process would insert deep-breathing techniques and intense concepts, all of which were new to me. We would speak of the spirit, of the essence, but we always worked on the body more than on the mind. I saw people around me open up, laugh, and cry, but I viewed those reactions as forced, self-induced feelings, not true.

One day, music was used to accompany the usual exercises, movements, and breathing. After a good hour of work, I felt that something was moving inside me, and although I tried to control it, I could not identify what it was and why it was happening.

I just knew that some big, slow, warm tears were involuntarily beginning to fall. At the end of the warm-up, four people went up on stage to perform a scene. Every single word and expression of the actors hit me as if I didn't have any skin; their every breath and gesture vibrated in me with a piercing effect, and I felt the urge to leave the room, like when the feeling of wanting to throw up rises rapidly and you flee to the restroom. I ran to the next room, doubled over, where I threw up emotions and memories directly from my body, from my belly. In the eye of the storm, the only thing clear and meaningful to me was that I was freeing myself from all that had prevented me from really relating to myself and to my life. I continued to cry and release emotions for about forty-eight hours. Back at the Stanislavski workshop, I later discovered that the techniques and the songs were "borrowed" from yoga. Soon after, I entered the first Hatha Yoga school I could find and practiced for a few months, until I met a former Kundalini Yoga teacher and asked her to teach me. During my first Kundalini Yoga class, the same music that had been used in the acting workshop was played, and I noticed that the breathing techniques belonged to Kundalini Yoga as well.

In that Kundalini Yoga class, I finally felt completely synchronized: I was where I needed to be, and I was doing the only thing there was to be done, the right thing at the right time. And yet this change in my life brought on its own confusion and emotions. As I learned more and more about Kundalini Yoga, I continued to work in acting. One day I went to an audition—which I still rank as my worst audition ever—and due to my utter confusion and highly emotional state, I was unable to remember the script; I left feeling like a complete failure. Surprisingly, two months later, I was called to interpret the lead character. Insecure but happy, I hesitated at first and then accepted the part. I left immediately for

Morocco, where I stayed for the two months of filming. And yet the extraordinary thing was not that I had been chosen, with all the consequences that entailed; the extraordinary thing was the role I had to play. My then-partner, who knew me very well, said the role represented a perfect picture of myself.

The film was set in ancient Egypt, and I had to play the role of twin brothers, sons of the pharaoh and the queen who, for political reasons, are separated at birth. They grow up in two different environments, with different education and stimuli, unaware of the other's existence. The child who remains with the pharaoh is considered the rightful heir to the throne. He is a young prince and a great warrior, strong, determined, and irresistible. The other grows up with a master astrologer and becomes his disciple. He is a spiritual person, contained, intuitive, incapable of harming a living being, humble, and devoted to meditation. They represent two extremes, two opposites, two sides of the same coin, and they meet just before the prince dies in the arms of his brother. From here, the surviving brother gradually discovers the truth of who he is and underoes a long process to find the courage to develop his brother's qualities. His challenge is in harmonizing the two opposites, the two lobes of a single brain, into a single human being who will be able to inherit the leadership necessary to govern the kingdom and bring wisdom, peace, and prosperity to the land.

In me, these two polarities were clearly visible to the director's eye and to my partner, who, in her own skin, knew my conflict between the saint and the warrior and the impact of this conflict on my behavior. I had just started practicing Kundalini Yoga. While studying its origins and its history, I learned that the technology of Kundalini Yoga reached an epochal evolution when it came in close contact with the Sikh tradition. The Sikhs took this form of royal yoga (Raja Yoga), which had been practiced only by ascetics and royalty, and enriched it with their tradition, enabling its disclosure to the common man, the householder. The Sikh tradition is that of the saint–warrior—men and women who, in their everyday lives, express spiritual and temporal strength, devotion, and the ability to act; their service, excellence, and commitment are unwavering.

A few days after I arrived on set, I began to understand and accept the value of the message inherent in what was happening to me. My groping attempts at excelling seemed more the result of naivety than of mistakes. In addition, the time I had spent groping didn't seem lost; rather, it felt more like a prerequisite for getting me to see what life had in store for me. I was clearly being directed toward something—with big road signs! From my depths, I heard an echo of almost impalpable feelings related to my childhood resonate with this perception, now clear and vivid. I recognized the innocent experience of inner calm from my early youth. Today I would describe it like this: I was feeling completely myself. Innocence provided a direct experience of the known and the unknown, at the same time. The lack of superstructure and personality of those feelings allowed me to dive farther into the unknown.

After completing filming, while still in that ancestral land of deserts, oases, smells, and people, I felt like a child who has to leave the place where he was born. My home, my work, all my familiar places, environments, and relationships seemed distant and suspended, like a dream. In that heavy air, far from home, I decided to follow the vision. Yoga became the purpose, and acting became the medium. A couple of decades later, I found this quote by Yogi Bhajan that best describes my mood at that time, and that still resonates within me during big changes in my life:

So the caravan moves on and the winds bring the morning message and the dew tells the night is on his way out and the travelers look to the journey through the bright burning sun to the sand dunes till another moon comes and comforts for the night.[4]

Drib Drishti Kriya to Show You the Future

September 22, 1986

Part I: Lotus Mudra at the Heart Center. Bring the heels of the hands together with the tips of the thumbs and the tips of the pinkie fingers touching, the other fingers are spread evenly. Close the eyes and look down to the center of the mudra behind closed eyes. Chant, "I am, I am, myself is not for sale," in a monotone for **1 minute**.

Part II: Bring your hands just above the eyebrows, palms down, as if you were shading your eyes. Thumbs and fingers are straight and together, the fingers point toward each other and remain about an inch apart. The hands don't touch the face. Look straight ahead and chant, very methodically, not too fast: Har Haray Haree. **2 minutes.**

Part III: Keep your hands above the eyebrows, but allow the thumbs to drop down. Continue to look straight ahead. Using the mantra, Har Haray Haree Whaa Hay Guroo, chant aloud Har Haray Haree and then press the navel in toward the spine. Then chant silently Whaa Hay Guroo. Then release the navel and begin the sequence again. These two mantras should be done in 4 beats each; they should balance each other. Do not exceed **31 minutes.**

Comments: This secret kriya will remove your fear of the future. You know what the future is? This kriya allows you to start seeing the future; it brings you the future today. If this kriya becomes perfect, your future will always be known to you. In fact, if you do this kriya, the future will not only be known, but also that part of you which is negative in the future will be eliminated; only a token shall remain. For example, you were to lose an arm in an accident. When the accident takes place you receive only a scratch. Instead of losing an arm you may have a little cut.

Chapter Two

The Courage

To Attempt It and to Keep Up

As we capture the vision in the midst of the unknown, we are left surprised and elated at the same time. If, at that time, our analytical, practical mind takes into consideration the ocean that separates us from carrying it out, then the vision will seem like an unlikely hypothesis. If, however, we see the vision as pure potentiality, then the contents of the vision will resonate with the uniqueness of our frequency. This resonance gives us not only an instant sense of who we are, but also the opportunity to express and expand ourselves.

When pursuing a goal, we tend to see only a partial or general vision of our true selves in action—a single frame of a fraction of our lives. The breadth and depth of the details that we see depend not only on the exposure time for which the shutter of our perceptive system's camera is open but also on the film's sensitivity. The vision of the objectives of specific phases of our life—or of our entire life— imprints itself in our consciousness in proportion to how much we identify with those objectives. Basically the more we see, the more we awaken to ourselves, and, if we choose to believe what we see, we can set an intention. Revealing its will through the vision, our soul encourages us to follow it. Our identification with this intention creates an invigorating chemical reaction: Our life force begins to flow. We feel motivated, and we start reaching toward the realization of what is now just a seed of creativity in our psyche.

During rock climbing, when your body is trembling and your sensitivity is restricted by stress and fear, you spend your last energy gluing yourself to the rock and stretching your neck in search of a possible foot- or handhold. In that trembling moment, if you don't accept what is happening to you, it will be hard for you to find the burst of courage to leave your safe support for an uncertain one. Even if you find that courage, there will be a moment when, by just a few inches, you will have left the place in which you were without yet reaching the place where you are going. You're in between, in a void, in the unknown. At that moment, the reaction of your nervous system and the new chemistry in your glands will spark an inner explosion. Whether you end up at the top where you hoped to be or down where you were afraid of falling, it makes no difference—the important thing is that you tried. Simply by trying, you allowed your subconscious to register the way in which your fears can be overcome or at least confronted. The unknown space on which you had built your fears will become known.

Life hasn't been given to us to be lived in fear. Every intention born out of fear is essentially wrong from the start. There is a boundary, as thin as a knife blade, that divides truth from lies and fact from fantasy. Every time we let our mind go on automatic, every time we lack awareness, we are slipping on that blade. When the mind is not committed to serving the consciousness, our mental intrigues play their usual games—the same games that, time after time, have separated us or distanced us from the soul's priorities and potentialities. When we believe in the mind's games instead of the soul's truth, we depend on a thought, on the visible and the tangible, rather than believing in the unlimited and the invisible within us. To pass from dependence to independence—which is what this is—requires courage.

Although I allowed my vision to set me on the path of yoga, the decision to dedicate my time and space to this practice did not resolve my previous situation. All the conflicts in my professional and social life still remained alive—though weakened—leaving no room for the potential courage I was flaunting. Using the pretext of these persisting difficulties, I flew across the ocean to sit at my Master's feet and offer him my intentions and motives. Being at the feet of the Master is like being naked in front of your own consciousness. His presence is a mirror that accurately reflects the distance between you and who you could be and that clearly shows you how you resist being yourself. As I listed all my difficulties, challenges, frictions in relationships, and complications at work, my discomfort grew more and more, because I became increasingly aware that my speech was ill founded. By stating my grievances out loud, I could obtain anyone's sympathy and condolences—even my own—but not his. Until then, everyone I'd chosen to speak to had a precise weakness in their psyche that was receptive to my frequency, and they would always endorse my arguments and behavior in order to justify their own. After all, a trouble shared is a trouble halved. Until then, I had always "won," but this time I had trapped myself. To awake from the dream, I had chosen the Master as my audience.

A Master highlights all of your nonsense and brings you back to reality. Like a serial killer who wants to be found and stopped, I was desperate enough to talk to the Master. Within a few moments, I realized I was handing myself over to truth; I was tired of the lies I had been telling myself. The result was painful but cathartic. I courageously announced that I wanted to leave my city and my work to start over somewhere else, unaware that by doing so I was hiding behind the excuse of a spiritual path. My Master was very blunt, penetrating, and unconditional: I had to find, consolidate, and express myself in the mud I had already created, in those relationships and through those difficulties. Nurtured by yoga, I would have to teach it and build my life according to the teachings themselves. Those who were provoking me were a blessing and a tool for growth, and each difficulty was an opportunity to excel.

Is courage staying when you want to go and going when you want to stay? I realized that even if disguised as courage, my idea to leave and start over was not a chance to begin anew; rather, it was an attempt to escape. This pattern had been typical in my life—wearing my backpack, I was always ready to leave as soon as things got bad. I had always been effective at breaking things up and starting fresh somewhere else. But each time I moved on, I hadn't realized that any unresolved issues would weigh a ton on my future and that all these same dynamics would return to manifest themselves again in a different shape. The other people I encountered were only extras on the scene directed by my paradigms.

The intensity of what happens to us sometimes becomes so strong that it cannot be contained and, consequently, lived. If our nervous system cannot contain the experience, we will be driven by our impulsiveness and act according to our mental intrigues. We will do anything rather than be under that pressure and that suffering, and above all, we will do anything not to face the unknown. At the height of the challenge, we will have only two choices: to fight or to flee. But neither of these options has anything to do with courage. Tolerance alone creates a condition in which the heart's mind and the mind's heart work together to give courage. Tolerance is essential for staying in the reality of our experiences and our relationships— relationships with ourselves, our partners, the mountain, our God. Whether the experience is joyful or heartbreaking, tolerance allows us to live it fully. Trying to avoid the resulting pain does nothing but keep it alive. When we allow ourselves to look into the eyes of the tiger and hold its gaze, we realize that the tiger in our mind is always more ferocious than the one standing before us. When we can tolerate the unthinkable, courage will begin to flow into our life force, and we will take one step toward the unknown—where we had never allowed ourselves to go before—where we will know more about ourselves.

Most of the time, the choices we make are highly predictable and rarely elevating; more often than not, they are reactions to circumstances. The fear of confronting ourselves pushes us to move, to escape, rather than contacting our courage and tolerating the experience. But when at the height of tension, we are firm in spirit and have the courage to go through what is happening, our subconscious registers that courage, and life itself will help us by giving us a priceless sense of security. The path that requires more courage is our own. The biggest challenge lies in dealing with the unknown that hides behind fear. It is only through facing this challenge that we can realize there is no greater adventure than exploring the unknown within us. In Yogi Bhajan's words:

> *Your soul has a fundamental property that, when aligned with your mind, gives you impact, intelligence, and effectiveness. Its fundamental property is to be saibhang—a self-illumined, aware, and radiant identity of God. It is not subject to anything. This has been a known fact, explored and experienced for centuries. The soul is a slave to none. In fact, everything else is subject to the soul and connected through its projection. So if you call on that and dwell in that, it works where no logic, reason, or mental intrigue can.[5]*

If tolerance is the mother of courage, then compassion is the father. Tolerance and compassion help us transform our passion from an intensity that is only interested in satisfying our ego to a fire motivated to serve broader purposes and to be more farsighted and more understanding of others. We must cultivate a passion for making our lives useful by bringing well-being and prosperity to all who surround us. Tolerance leads to a neutral state, where our ability to contain becomes impartial. We can experience polarity and opposites without the preconceptions of right and wrong. Our mind and our being find an inner silence in which a calm, peaceful clarity clearly shows us who we are. Silence, or shuniya, is the condition from which everything becomes possible; it is the emptiness on which excellence is nourished and in which it dwells. From this clarity and feeling of fullness, compassion becomes possible. Tolerating ourselves, having compassion, and cultivating silence are the first steps toward gaining courage.

Two driving forces alternate with each other in guiding our choices: love and fear. When fear is hovering over a situation, we may attempt to push it away, to make it into a transient condition. In reality, however, if fear is not processed or handled with courage, it remains suspended over us. It hangs like a shadow, a veil of uncertainty in our image of ourselves as free individuals. That uncertainty undermines our decisions and our intentions. Our basic tendency is to stop what doesn't seem manageable; doing so gives us the illusion that we have freed ourselves from it. But, in fact, we are only postponing the problem. For example, the fear of passing time brings us ever closer to death. Unable to stop time, we have learned to suspend our problems in the belief that we are gaining living space; but we are only reducing the quality of our vision. So we end up living in a small square surrounded by all that we have suspended. The time between the suspension and the next relapse of our fear is always imbued with the flavor of that specific fear and the consequences it brings. When faced with fear, there are two options: suspend or attend. Courage is to attend.

With courage, even if we are overwhelmed by fear, we can face the situation and go through it. Courage does not eliminate the fear, but it is the process through which we can learn that fear does not exist. Fear is imaginary; it is the result of fantasies and preconceptions. Fear is the idea of what could happen, and it's caused by our sense of separation from others and from everything. Having courage is different from being fearless. We are fearless when we feel every cell vibrating infinity and when we feel infinity within. Everything that exists and everything that doesn't exist is within. This idea is called *Ang Sang Wahe Guru:* "The dynamic, living ecstasy of the universe is dancing within every cell of me." Until we reach this awareness, however, we need courage to bridge the gap between the vision and its achievement, between the vision and the strategy to achieve it.

When I returned to my own city after completing the filming in Morocco, I found all my unresolved challenges waiting for me. For example, I increasingly suffered the constant exposure to an audience always ready to judge. I was influenced by the idea of having to do well and having to act as expected. Even though this shadow presented only a minimum distraction, it was as annoying as a stone in my shoe; it influenced me to the point of producing an inner conflict that I pretended not to see. Later in my life, while teaching Kundalini Yoga, I found myself in front of many more people than ever before, exposing myself more than I ever dreamed of doing in fashion and movies. I was doing this more consistently but also with less mercy from the audience. The audience does not expect much in terms of personal life, ethical values, and consistency between an actor's words on screen and his actions in real life; being an artist justifies many things. Lifestyle teachers, however, should set an example for their audience. If people find a flaw, it justifies them in their decision to stay where they are. My repressed fear of having to be a certain way reappeared in my new life so arrogantly, but this time it was in a context in which I felt (and feel) such love and conviction to move and act from the real me, to serve at my best. A natural flow of healthy courage was able to dissolve any initial fear.

You cannot hide from your fears. There is no way to be comfortable if love and gratitude for life are not with you. If the vision is true, though the path may not be easy, convenient, and fearless, it will be yours, and the courage you put into it will lead you to yourself. Without a vision, however, you don't have any alternative but to stay in the frame of your fear. Without courage, you can't turn your vision into your mission. In my case, I chose to carry out my Master's mission, and I have been honored by this opportunity. After all, I am just passing on his teachings. I am serving something beyond myself, and this offers a deep meaning to my life's purpose and direction.

Conquering One's Imagined Disabilities

April 15, 1993

Every disability is imagined. Every achievement is an experience. This kriya develops our own human courage to overcome our imagined disabilities.

⌐ Yogi Bhajan

1. Sit in Easy Pose with a straight spine. Bend the elbows so that the upper arms are near the ribcage and the forearms point upward. The hands start out in front of the shoulders with the fingers spread. The palms face outward and the thumbs point at each other. Twist the wrists inward with the thumb leading the way until the palms face the body and the thumbs point out to the sides. As the wrists twist inward, the fingers close into a fist. They re-open as the wrists twist outward to return to the starting

position. Make your mouth into an **"O" shape and begin a panting dog breath** through the open mouth. The wrists twist in time with the breath. Move quickly. Look at the tip of the nose. **3 minutes.** This exercise can bring great healing to the body.

To End: Inhale, hold the breath 15-20 seconds, tighten the fingers into fists and tense every muscle in the body. Exhale. Repeat this sequence two more times and relax.

2. Begin alternately pushing the arms and hands forward as if you were pushing something away from you. Push one hand out as the other pulls back along your side. Keep the hands and fingers

open letting the heel of the palm lead the movement. **Make an "O" of the mouth and do a panting dog breath through the open mouth.** This exercise will work out your blocks. **3 minutes.**

To End: Inhale, keep one arm extended while you hold the breath 15-20 seconds and squeeze all the muscles of the body. Exhale. Inhale, extend the other arm while you hold the breath 15-20 seconds and tighten all your muscles. Exhale and relax.

3. Open your arms wide with your elbows slightly bent, the fingers spread open and the hands slightly cupped. Move your arms in backwards circles as you do a **panting dog breath through the "O" shaped mouth.** Move vigorously. **3 minutes.** This benefits the heart.

To End: Inhale, stick your tongue out to the maximum, hold the breath 15-20 seconds and tense the entire body so much that it shakes from tension. Exhale. Repeat twice more.

Chapter Three

The Grit

To Go Through It

You have mustered up the courage to move into the unknown and follow your vision. Now you're like a warrior fighting for the freedom to be yourself. You're fighting with you and for you, to overcome your fears, your subconscious, your nonsense. From a hole in your paradigm, you saw the potential you, and you answered the call: You challenged your fears, and it was like defying death. Now you're in limbo, waiting. Underfoot you no longer have the ground you knew; instead, if the subconscious world is spying on you from behind the scenes, projecting your own insecurities. But you begin to believe that if you move forward, cardboard walls, trees, and ghosts will fall, giving way to a new environment, imbued with your essence and co-created by the reflection of your courageous projection. This phase has no fixed term, and the challenges and situations within it are not quantifiable. Courage gave you the impetus to confront what seemed impossible, but now, in the succession of events that you allowed to converge toward you, you need grit in order to have continuity, strength, and effectiveness.

Grit can only be accessed if the new context of life is a direct result of a courageous action or decision. On this path toward excellence, grit is necessary to keep the vision alive in our consciousness, as events and pressures frequently and intensely test us to see how dedicated and committed we are to our own cause. If, on the other hand, we were to persevere in fear, we would not need grit; all we would need is a continued denial of ourselves and a submission to the circumstances. No matter how much support we receive from the universe, from someone who decides to stand with us, or from our very own being, according to the simple law of polarity, a force equal and opposite to that support will challenge us on our path toward excellence. It took courage to decide we wanted to win; now grit gives us the strength to persist. When fatigue, pressure, and discomfort manifest themselves, grit is the stamina that urges our essence to keep up, our body not to give up, and our mind to remain focused on our purpose so that we don't sacrifice the vision and thwart our initial courage. The vision is our goal and our mission; if we sacrifice it, we are corrupt.

Any decision or choice that is against our mission can be defined as corruption—it has been polluted by fear or it was a decision made because we were seeking momentary gratification in an attempt to escape from confronting our fear. When we search for happiness in the usual areas of ego, status, and comfort, we are deceiving ourselves. The satisfaction we seek lies not in the temporary relief of escaping fear but in overcoming it with love, fulfilling ourselves, and elevating others. Without this kind of satisfaction, we become emotional, neurotic, and competitive. To avoid this, we must have grit to remind ourselves that we are serving our soul's purpose, rather than the needs of our personality and ego. Grit gives us the strength not to react, while, at the same time, giving us the power and strength to continue in spite of everything, faithful to an idea. The powerful projection of reality cannot be killed, scarred, or corrupted. Grit is you, beyond all doubt. As Yogi Bhajan said,

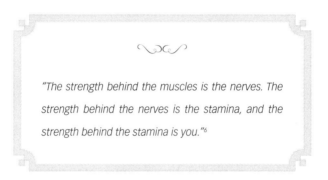

"The strength behind the muscles is the nerves. The strength behind the nerves is the stamina, and the strength behind the stamina is you."[6]

Throughout our lives, we face the usual dilemma: how to decide on or remember what it is we want to serve. Each moment, we define our destiny by drifting away from or getting closer to our fate. The power to choose what to serve and whether to be in truth is inherent in our free will. The intention we decide to serve will determine our direction, depth, and vibration. To relate to truth is to keep on the path that links us to our mission and our destiny, but this is not possible without self-respect. If we have no self-respect or self-knowledge, we will never be able to relate to truth— as wonderful or terrible as that truth may be—because we won't feel able to cope with it. This is where it starts getting painful. Lack of self-respect and the inability to show grit come from our imprinting, from our first years of life.

The greatest thing I was taught is that I have a complete, full, isolated but sovereign identity. That only your mother can give you. You can't get that in any other way. Your sovereignty can only be given to you as a child by your mother, by identifying you as a complete, total individual. And what you call grit, strength of the identity, is given to you by your father. And it is all done in the first eleven years. Afterward, anything said or done and taught is useless. Anything thereafter is a matter of knowledge; the base is already built.[7]

The transference of self-respect from our mothers and grit from our fathers occurs in the formative relationship between parents and children, just as we assimilate minerals from the water we drink. Strong self-respect gives rise to self-reverence, which spurs us to honor and elevate ourselves through any condition. The teachings of Kundalini Yoga recognize and accept the law that a cause will generate specific effects and consequences; the teachings brilliantly use this law not only as a diagnostic tool to trace the nature of a particular dysfunction, but also to promote certain purposes, as far and improbable as they may seem. Each new attitude creates the conditions to encourage the proliferation of other attitudes. Whether we are moving toward expansion or toward contraction, the process is the same, though the attitudes are different.

Giving ourselves the possibility of having elevated attitudes promotes an aptitude for higher purposes. Mental silence, openness, and perception are the conditions for obtaining the vision. Tolerance and compassion are the conditions for experiencing courage. Self-respect and self-reverence are the conditions necessary to show grit. Just as small grapes grow and form a bunch, weighing down the branch that feeds them and helping give uniqueness to the entire plant's shape, our attitudes, the intensity with which we feel, and the qualities we express give each of us our own uniqueness. The result of all of this lies not only in the shape our identity takes, but also in the flavor, strength, and intensity with which the soul manifests through us and in the delicacy of the fruit we deliver. The harmony with which this happens gives testimony to our grace.

As long as our subconscious is inhabited by the same patterns, our frequency will vibrate in the same way, and, like a magnet, we will attract situations that lead us to measure ourselves, time after time, with the unresolved. Each new situation, person, environment, and purpose, though different, will be spoiled by the same inclination. This applies to relationships, work, and health. Once I had decided to start my life over in the place from which I wanted to escape, in that old amalgam that I had built with my own actions, I had to motivate myself with new goals and new tools. My first lesson was understanding the difficulties we all have in accepting responsibility for our actions, especially those of the past, because our concept of freedom leads us to run away from those actions. The karma we have created and the dynamics it unleashes cannot be misled; they will track us down anywhere until we pay it off, and, with grace, we either understand or transcend them. The courage to confront what we still do not know will manifest the known that has not yet been resolved. At that same time, I learned my second lesson: Courage, once obtained, needs to be found again and again and to be supported and extended by grit. Life shows us how that, without grit, fate undermines the courage we have shown in order to reach our destiny. I have found that sooner or later, we all must learn these two fundamental lessons; otherwise, even if we change circumstances, places, and people, our tendencies and dynamics will remain the same.

So, I had returned to the context that I had helped build, but this time with the understanding that I could change it only in proportion to how much I was willing to change myself. I thus was shifting the focus from outside to inside. In order for our lives to adapt to the needs and intentions of the soul, rather than being influenced by circumstances, we must know clearly who we are and what of ourselves we want to deliver and how. The change in my daily schedule, in my lifestyle, and in the discipline I was teaching and practicing gradually became incompatible with the social and personal relationships I had nurtured until then. The type of work I had done in the past had introduced me to many people who related to me, for the most part, through what I had been and what I had meant to them. They were tied to the image they had of me and that I had given them. But my inner change was gradually leading to a change in my appearance and in what I ate, said, and wanted. I learned that friends, colleagues, and even relatives often turn out just to be friends of our old habits; many of them resist any new attitudes that do not have their approval or that appear to undermine their security. Soon after I had returned home, many people began moving away from me, many situations started dissolving or transforming, and the dynamics started flowing in a different direction. At work, the usual sources of revenue were gradually decreasing. In relationships, those who stood by me, but who felt somewhat betrayed by my change, started showing their discontent. From the moment I decided to follow my Master's order, my intention started doing its work, and I watched as the set I had previously arranged with great care gradually collapsed all around me. The people around us who undermine or delay our changes are nothing but branches and projections of ourselves, and they must either be honored and left to go gracefully or be gracefully embedded in our evolution.

My life at that time resembled a city that had been repeatedly bombed and then razed to the ground, with only a few buildings left standing. From the ruins, I could see how much and in what way I could rebuild and, at the same time, what I was sacrificing to do this. In the midst of this difficult process, strength and enthusiasm seemed to sometimes sneak away with the security I thought I had. Events can turn for the worse, and the vision is likely to be forgotten, bartered, or removed, unless grit comes in to take over the field.

The overwhelming feeling of that period and the very image of the collapsed city came up again several years later, when, after having purchased some land and a house in the countryside, I began a renovation project of the old building, which eventually led to its demolition and complete reconstruction. After a thousand bureaucracies, permits, and projects and after having demolished the old house and put in the ground pillars for the new foundation structure, all work was halted for about eighteen months because of a new seismic safety law. The law resulted in a large expenditure of money to keep the building to code, as well as new permits and further delay. I was so frustrated that I avoided going to the site all together. Then, one winter day, I went to the site and saw that the rain and frost had replaced the foundations of the house with a frozen lake. There was no trace of all the investment of energy, money, and time; only a wasteland marked by the tracks left by the builders' machinery, and a bare tree here and there. But I had been made stronger by my previous experience of having reinvented my life, so my recovery upon seeing the devastated site was more rapid. I recognized more easily that gaining the courage and boldness necessary to complete such a project required a shift, an antidote to failure, an attitude immune to demotivation: It required grit.

Today, where there was once a frozen lake, there is now a beautiful, nearly complete house. No one knows everything that has happened to reach the current state; they cannot see how much mud has been shoveled, how much iron has been inserted, or what the foundations and the water pipes look like. Nor can they see the difficulties and joys experienced. But I can see it all, and that feeling is priceless.

The experience of remaining faithful to our vision, regardless of circumstances, difficulties, hardships, and physical and mental exhaustion, becomes a solid foundation in our subconscious. Eighty percent of what happens within us after we've had the courage to start or leave something is unknown to us—it depends on the Infinite. Ten percent depends on others (the counterparty), and the remaining ten percent depends on us. The unknown that we choose to see is unpredictable, surprising, and incomprehensible.

If we do not achieve what we expect or want, we end up fighting against the achievement of our vision. In doing so, we ignore how every vicissitude that confronts us brings us one step closer to realizing the vision—and therefore ourselves. Instead of facing reality, we argue with reality, because we are slaves to our yardstick and our fantasies. From where do we draw the strength to stay committed to realizing our vision without being surprised or caught off-guard by what will happen in the future—be it poverty, misfortune, or the most phenomenal of fears? The first prerequisite is to be free, in the most real and absolute sense. We are free only if we accept *everything* that happens, not only that which our beliefs and paradigms think possible. When we fail to deal with and measure ourselves against what we do not accept, circumstances end up prevailing upon us, and our complaints end up stifling our grit.

The second necessary strength to have is the power to sacrifice. The vicissitudes that keep us from the top of the mountain are a passage as narrow as the eye of a needle. We have to sacrifice prejudice, pride, and frustration in order to pass through the eye of that needle. We have to sacrifice the superfluous and our notion of safety. We have to risk having nothing but our own skin.

Ultimately, the final thing that makes it possible for us to give up our deepest fears and most attractive temptations is love. Without love, there is no reason to sacrifice. Without love, sacrifice is death; but with love, sacrifice becomes life. If your love for the mountain, for life, and for yourself—and your willingness to help others and to set an example of how to be free and realized—does not prevail, why go through all that?

In climbing, when you follow a path already marked with preplaced equipment, getting to the top in Italian is called *chiudere una via,* or "closing a route" When you set a new path and find a vertical way to the top, it is called *aprire una via,* or "opening a route." There is a big difference between the two. In the first case, you already know the path and have studied it and maybe even practiced it before. But even if you've climbed the same route many times, you may find it difficult to climb today due to variations in your psycho-physical abilities or in the weather. As in life, certain situations may be difficult, even if you've faced them before. It may happen that after finding the courage to take a step, the next steps feel progressively worse, leaving you out of breath or undermining your strength and morale. Other times, you may want to hold the grip to move up, but your hands are no longer able to move, your fingers cannot get close to each other, your arms won't stretch any higher, your feet tremble on the foothold, and you wonder what you're doing and why you went so far, reminding yourself not to do it ever again. It may be that once on top, you are so exhausted that you can't pass the rope in the final hook and come down again. Nobody forces you to climb; it's not about life or death, but once you are hung up there, your fear of whether you will live or die is violently highlighted, along with your dynamics and the opportunities available for you to escape or win. And that's why you do it—you are training yourself to live and die with dignity and grace.

So too in life—routes that are still to be opened carry with them the unknown possibility of becoming feasible. If you create a new path, you are a pioneer—you are tracing the coordinates on which others can train themselves. As for the safety of opening a route, the risk is different from that in climbing a known route: With the former, you cannot be secured from below until you secure your own self from within. In addition, the attitude is different; because there is no trail to follow, you have to be fully present and aware enough to allow your creativity and intuition to flow and guide you. Even if you are doing it for sport, even if the difficulty is a fake difficulty, when you are there, everything becomes real: Without love for your goal, for your means, and for adventure, grit will not surface.

Etymologically, grit comes from *grimta,* which means "rage, anger, temper." Therefore, grit usually means being motivated by anger to reach out to achieve a goal or a victory pushed for. But this type of propellant provides only short bursts of energy and implies a reactivity that is rarely a good counselor. But when love is used as a propellant, it is inexhaustible and leads us to achievement through actions of awareness. Grit is difficult to obtain, but if it is founded on love, it testifies to a stable and high level of awareness. It closes the first triad of the Elements of Excellence: vision, courage, grit.

When our insecurities are laid bare, grit allows us to tap into our deepest inner resources and test the strength of our foundations. And yet this is the moment when many of us decide to remain in mediocrity. In your past relationships, how many times during the deepest crises, after having the courage to enter the relationship, did you show enough grit to persevere until you reached new levels of quality? How many times did you give up or remain stuck, avoiding the pressure and trying to limit the damage?

We don't need to find ourselves hanging on a wall or to question our whole life, just as we don't need to find ourselves in a relationship with another individual. Let's ask ourselves instead how much grit we have in relation to ourselves and to being who we are. External relationships, challenges, and life will get stuck where we are stuck in ourselves, and they will shine where, with love and grit, we have conquered our own mind.

Meditation for Self Control

November 7, 1999

Part I: Cross Your Barrier

Sit straight in a cross-legged position. Lock your hands in Bear Grip in front of the forehead, with elbows out to the side. Make an "O" of your mouth and inhale through the mouth and raise the hands, straightening the arms above the head. Exhale through the nose and return to the starting position. Close the eyes and meditate on the sound of the breath. Continue for **3 minutes.** To end, inhale deeply, hold, stretch the hands up and lengthen the spine. Cannon Fire exhale. Relax.

Move very systematically and rhythmically so that all disease can be burned out of the blood. Listen to the sound of the Breath of Life – this can do more for you than the movement. Become part of the total energy. Do not lose courage. Test your grit. Cross the barrier! These exercises are re-vibrating and re-shaping your being with the Breath of Life. We are doing them to break that line beyond which you cannot go. To cross that limited space to become unlimited. To cross that defined state of mind to become Infinite.

PART II: Shiva Shakti Kriya

Bring the hands together in front of the mouth in Lotus Bud Mudra: the fingertips and the base of the hands are touching, creating a ball shape, thumbs are together. Elbows are relaxed down. Make an "O" of the mouth and inhale and exhale through the mouth. Inhale as the thumbs (the lingam, the male organ) go inside the space between the hands (the yoni, the female organ). Exhale and extend the thumbs toward the mouth. Continue for **3 minutes.** Any time you do this exercise it will energize you and your physical health.

PART III: Recharge

Raise both arms to 60 degrees with no bend in the elbows, palms face forward, and fingers are spread open and tight like steel. The tighter the fingers are, the more perfectly the energy will prevail. Make an "O" of your mouth and breathe through the mouth with full strength. Receive energy from the heavens and earth to recharge and become strong. Continue for **3 minutes**. To end, inhale deeply, hold, and let this breath circulate through your being. Cannon Fire exhale. Relax.

Comments: You need to be in your own control. If you practice this meditation, it will help you.

You can do these three exercises each morning in bed to revive and renew yourself for the whole day. And the whole day you can be charming, energetic, together and real. Knowledge belongs to those who practice, and lousiness belongs to those who do not. Knowing is not enough. Experience is.

Chapter Four

The Humility

To Know Who the Doer Is

The ability to progress and to contain our progress develops in proportion to our level of awareness. If limited, our level of awareness allows only partial and incomplete achievements. Unless the mind becomes vast and unless awareness dwells on infinite horizons, we remain restricted in our limited range. Containing and coexisting with ourselves already involves an intense amount of responsibility. Once we add roles and relationships, containment becomes insufficient, like the roots of a single tree that cannot give firmness to the land of an entire hill. Coexistence ends up feeling like a crowded aquarium that doesn't have enough living space or nutrients for its many fish.

As human beings, we fully recognize this limitation, and we experience it as a grief from which there seems to be no way out. When we feel the pain this causes us, either we cover it up and deny it, or we delve into it completely, as if it were the only thing happening, the only possible reality. We are like champions who win but cannot handle success, fame, and notoriety; like an athlete who shows the potential in training to be a champion, but fails to win when it comes time to play the game.

In drama school, I saw the best actors in the world, the most thrilling scenes, and the truest feelings. The intensity and accuracy of the interpretations were not approximate reproductions of moods, but complete identifications, with the complexity and reality of each character enriched by the creativity of improvisation. I witnessed actors who could draw out the soul's light by penetrating the darkest corners of the subconscious mind, using only a smell, a picture, or a feeling as access keys. And yet, an insignificant percentage of these people became successful actors. In front of the mirror, everyone is talented; but faced with the pressure of the audition, things often change.

I have come to recognize that the test we face in trying to achieve our goal is not the momentary pressure of the challenge itself, which can be overcome with a little training; rather, it is the responsibility of what follows. Achieving success in the business, social, or temporal world doesn't necessarily mean we are able to contain it and keep it. In truth, every achievement involves, as in a marriage, a responsibility. We can be inebriated by our vision; we may experience the thrill of courage, the ardor of grit, or even the achievement of our goal, but to progress toward excellence and honor, to complete and magnify what we have achieved, we need an infinite perspective to give us stimulus and amplitude.

How much can our nervous system contain as it goes on relating and expanding? How much pressure can we manage before it turns into stress? How can we overcome fear and merge with our achievement? I always fought to win something with the intent, at heart, of becoming part of it. But often, once victorious, I was tempted by a number of implications that convinced me to destroy what I had achieved. Other times, I failed to honor the conquest, degrading it or keeping it on a level of mediocrity. And still other times, foreseeing the responsibilities that would come with achieving my goal and feeling the expectations of others, I didn't fight at all—or rather, I pretended to fight in order to have an excuse for failure.

These first experiences of mine trace the profile of a coward king, whose only nobility lay in his title. It may seem strange to relate to myself as a king, but the identity of the human being is full of sovereignty. Excellence means dwelling in reality through learning, obeying, and loving. Reality is the pivot around which our lives must revolve, the base from which we make our decisions and begin our relationships. Anything beyond this is a fantasy, a dream. The royalty I am talking about is the way we relate to reality by creating a standard of nobility and acting from that standard; it is a code of conduct that represents the soul's purity. Caliber is the ability to stay in reality, to confront the challenges that arise in order to project our own identity toward the Infinite. To access reality, we need to reset our preconceptions. To perceive reality, we need silence and sensitivity. To accept reality, we need flexibility. And to co-create with reality, we need creativity. Maintaining reality requires our constant and total presence so that integrity and dignity can flow in a consistent manner.

From where should we gather the power and impulse to put our whole selves into a project, a relationship, or a mission? Our innate sense of survival, which aims to avoid bankruptcy or suffering, can become a limit in those areas and occasions in which we should put all of ourselves with all sincerity. Humility is the answer. Without humility, we live in the belief that it's us acting, planning, conquering, taking care of consequences, and answering for our words, gestures, and tendencies. Being humble means feeling, recognizing, and accepting the only possible reality—that God is sitting next to us. If we are humble, we understand that the only source of everything going from us and coming to us is Infinity. When we are humble, we understand that we have no power to act, to comprehend, to speak, to have, or to reject. We align to the will of God, taking the exact mission that is required from us, until it becomes our will. When we do this, the power that flows through us, which is not ours, is indescribable. We can't even be proud of it; instead, we are infinitely grateful and honored to be its vehicle.

Kundalini Yoga teachings recognize God's will in this universal life blood that pervades us. God's will inspires us, moves us, and protects us. But to grasp this concept, we must have a predisposition to listen. Like radio waves, which have different frequencies, we can receive a signal only if we equalize and then reduce to silence all the other waves in our nervous system. The teachings call it *Hukam*— literally, a command—and it comes when we have ears to hear it and when we are ready to accept it in its totality.

For years, certain indecisions and dynamics left me in stand-by mode. I was engaged and present in life, but not one hundred percent. During a course, Guru Dev Singh, a teacher who I greatly respect and trust, introduced me to the students by saying, "He has a metaphysical problem—he is looking for the perfect Hukam." At first, his words seemed gratifying, and the people in the room interpreted them as a great compliment. Those words made me look like a surfer in search of the perfect wave, a mountain climber who lives for the perfect wall, or a bachelor waiting for his soul mate. In truth, however, I already knew that everything was perfect, that the opportunities available were perfect, and that I myself was perfect. Therefore, what at first sounded like a compliment suddenly shook me like a gong, waking me from the illusion that something would come to rescue me and show me the way. I was losing myself in concepts, ideas, sensations, and feelings and disguising my anxiety as devotion. I was hoping to see, in clear and detailed writing, what my mission was. In later years, I came to realize that events, relationships, and life itself were continually showing me the perfect Hukam that I was waiting for: Every path I resisted was where I had to go, and everything I disliked was what I had to learn to love.

Climbers use different grading systems to classify a route's difficulty and level of danger, and there is a phase, which is different for every climber, at which the parameters of approaching the rock change radically. For me, this phase comes after grade 6 (in the European grading system), which is when the rock is nearly vertical or overhanging and footholds and handholds become rare, requiring different approaches and dynamic moves. Climbing a grade 6 wall has nothing to do with grasping and pulling or pushing up; instead, it involves taking risks and using the thinnest vertical ledge as a useful step. Similarly, our way of thinking must change to find new and, until now, unimaginable physical laws, and it must surrender to nothing. The rock is right there, real and lapidary—we cannot change it. To tackle it, we need to create a level of consciousness that will help us perceive it not as an unsolvable problem but as an opportunity and a stimulus to creativity. Our own strength and abilities are no longer enough; we must rely on a divine support. For me, the rock became a bridge that would take me within myself, to a place from where I could observe who I was and who

I was going to be and feel pain and joy for both. Up on the rock, I experienced the void that came after my grit.

Actors or athletes are often defined as being "in a state of grace," meaning that their standards are above average human capacity. When in this state, these people trust the universe more than they trust themselves. They do not challenge nature or circumstances; instead, they merge with those circumstances in order to understand the mechanisms and flows. They do not fight; rather, they accept and allow. They transcend the problems and polarities, which do not affect them but instead encourage them. These people love not the action in itself; rather, they love to act according to God's will. Unknowingly, they are yogis, in that being a yogi is being humble. Nestled somewhere in our heart, we all have a memory of this state of grace. Every one of us, if only for a moment, has been a yogi.

When we are not humble, we become arrogant, inflated by thinking it is us who act. As strong, brave, and strategic as we may be, however, sooner or later, our limits will become manifest. Our actions aim to cover or fill the void we feel inside—they allow us to survive, but not to progress toward excellence. Humble is he who surrenders—not because of inferiority or incapacity, but because he recognizes that God acts through him. The humble being cancels his ego, which is hungry for recognition, and he does not worry, because he knows he is acting in partnership with or on behalf of the universe. This is the secret: Our limit is proportionate to our sense of separation, and our potential is proportionate to our sense of oneness with the Infinite itself.

The price to pay for humility is to sacrifice the ego's insanity. Until my encounter with yoga, I had been blocked by my own arrogance and pride. I had limited my intentions and my success to a narrow range and to the same scenario, like a leash around a dog's neck that confines him to the same backyard. During my adolescence—in sports, in school, in the fashion and movie business, and in my relationships—I rarely gave my best. On the rare occasions when I reached success, I made sure I disintegrated it. Everyone believed my excuses for this behavior, but I knew I was lying. Deep down I knew I refused to give my best so that I would not risk losing and suffering, or so that I would avoid taking responsibility for my victory.

In relationships, all of these limitations are amplified, because a relationship is a mirror in which we see our dynamics. In front of us we have another human being with dynamics that interweave and respond to our own, creating ever-changing geometries and games. In the past, I always started romantic relationships fired up with the idea of finding and touching the other person's soul. Without this prerequisite, it wasn't possible for me to start a relationship. Pushed or held back by this "all or nothing," I couldn't even think of relating to the opposite sex without the drive to conquer her completely. When the conditions were right and the contact occurred, my relationships would reach a peak radiance that always impressed me but later frightened me. I strongly felt the fear of not being able to have total control over what was happening, which, in fact, is impossible. After having conquered the land, plowed and fertilized it, and picked its first fruits, it was hard for me to lovingly start over and sow a new crop on the same plot. So I would flee the relationship, blaming boredom, the need for novelty, or my own inconsistency, thus causing suffering and anger to the wonderful women who had allowed me to have a relationship with them. In truth, my desire to love and to conquer was driven by my desire to connect my reality with the other person's reality, with the intention of creating a common reality, a true ground on which to live and be with the power of two in one. I had an idea of how I wanted my reality to be, based on what I wanted and what I was expecting. But in living together, the daily confrontation caused situations that I was not able to tolerate, and this prevented the next step: to live for each other.

At twenty-two, I married a wonderful woman, the mother of my first child. My dynamics, of which I was unconscious at the time but which were not justified by my young age, seemed clear to my wife, who was eleven years older than me. Over time, she decided to gradually loosen our relationship and eventually let me go. We maintained a good relationship throughout the years, and, eighteen years after of our separation, for my most recent birthday, she sent me a message: "We went searching for new adventures, because the ones we had we could no longer live in our hearts," citing, as is her style, the source: King Arthur to his knights of the Round Table. As I read the message, I nodded my head at his witty and precise message. A king always takes the core of the motivation that prompted him to expand, conquer, and win and shares it with his brave and loyal knights. In my relationship with my first wife, spirit, love, vision, grit, and courage had not been lacking, but I had not been able to accept the reality in which the achievements had taken shape.

When a woman is in love with a man, her life becomes a prayer for that man. And when a man is in love with a woman, he becomes humble. Although your greatest strength is love, it is not the love you know. In modern times, love provides only emotional co-existence. Men want to conquer women, and women want to conquer men. In reality, men and women should conquer Prakriti, the creativity around them, so that they can find a Creator beyond all layers.[8]

Often we abandon the situations that we created through actions, projections, and promises; we flee the situations in which we invested all our energy. What determines our inability to live in our hearts and experience the reality of love and life? The perceived impossibility of this reality is created by our fear that it may jeopardize our life force and limit our freedom. We refuse it because we do not understand it, and so we move toward other adventures.

The righteous king knows only one way—service. Once he obtains what he desired to conquer, he serves it with every possible and impossible resource: This is his code of nobility. Any of us can always move toward new adventures, but we should do so only in the spirit of continuing to serve our achievements with our entire self, like a righteous king. We can have anything we want to contain, and we can live in our heart—there is no limit. However, the key to doing so lies in our ability to serve. Serving makes something holy; serving is born out of love, and it produces love. The humble being, on bended knee, aligns his will to that of the Infinite and submits to its laws. The Infinite serves consistently, without prejudices and exclusions, its creation responding to the frequency of creation's vibrations. Serving the will of the Infinite, going beyond our inabilities, we can contain and deal with everything and everyone. When we allow ourselves to be humble, we are instantly able to see whether our zeal for conquest is based on a vision that deserves to be served because it is in line with the purpose of our higher self.

My Master knew that by sending me back into the life I had created with my past actions, he was showing me how to bow my head and be humble so that I could then shape my future differently. The fashion and movie business still held their doors open for me, even though those around me perceived my lack of enthusiasm toward those activities. So I decided to consider only those roles that would be interesting to me or that did not have too much visibility or that did not require changing my new appearance—my longer hair and unkempt beard. From one day to the next, I decided to cut off my work in fashion, which created a boomerang effect on a whole network of relations that I had been entertaining for some time. I was seen as a lunatic going through an existential crisis, because I was leaving a world that many longed for. Part of me, absorbing this process and hearing the comments, felt like everything was in a slow decay, in which beauty and charisma gradually fade. That part of me believed that my destructive nature was in full operational status. In contrast, however, the other part of me was thrown toward a future that was neither visible nor conceivable, but whose fragrance I'd glimpsed through my vision and Morocco's magic.

At that time, I was no longer what I always had been, but I was not yet what I would become. I was just a handful of molecules held together by the life force that extended from the consequences of the past and the intention of a future that laboriously planted its feet on the present moment. The invigorating effect secreted by my courage and grit had faded, and gradually I felt more and more like those in Gurudass Khalsa's poem:

> *Those who wait to be reborn*
> *in the glory of the Name*
> *They're like flowers in the rain*
> *waiting for the sun*
> *'Til their soul shall be reborn*
> *in the body of a saint*
> *who shall live forever*
> *in the hearts of those who love God.*

In addition to acting and fashion, my other job was as a teacher of gymnastics and stretching. The students who had been attending my classes for twenty years and who were very fond of me had no intention of stopping. But I was overcome by fatigue, because in addition to my gymnastics classes, the Kundalini Yoga classes I was teaching were multiplying. I was also homeless, thanks to the decline in revenue, so I slept a few hours a night in the gym. While traveling around the city to reach the different venues where I taught, I would make the most of even a few minutes and sleep in my parked car. Teaching gymnastics and stretching began to exhaust me, interacting with my students was becoming difficult, and fatigue reached me even when I was in full action. Yet I had a feeling that something was binding me to those classes, so I tried to apply yoga and patience to support me. I believed that my work was still incomplete, my relationship with it was not yet resolved, the karmic knot still had to untie. So I started wearing humility without even knowing what it was, agreeing to serve those people and situations until the circle was closed. This decision gave me a new stimulus. I served until I felt that my contribution and my work were no longer necessary and until I believed that someone else could replace me without my students feeling any difference. In that time, some people and situations evolved with me, and those who had become interested in yoga continued to relate to me, but in a different way.

One day, soon after I had started teaching Kundalini Yoga, I was alone in the classroom, cleaning the floor on my hands and knees. A young acting student, who resembled me in my earlier years, walked in and said, "I don't understand. Why do you do this when you could be a successful actor or a great teacher?" I remember feeling no anger or pride, because I knew that what I was doing was the right thing. This conscious transition made of patience, service, hard work, and trust was necessary for me. I felt an unknown force; it was different from what you feel when you can stop yourself in front of a temptation, higher than the respect you have of yourself, more genuine than when you receive great recognition: I was experiencing humility. Today, after a long time, I can firmly say that humility is the key, the only practical step, when situations seem impossible and pressure seems unsustainable. As Yogi Bhajan said,

"Mastery comes with humility, not ego. If one of you can conquer personal ego, which is very easy to do, the universe can be at your feet."[9]

Meditation on the Essence of Consciousness [10]

1. Sit in Easy Pose, with the hands in Gyan Mudra. The tip of the first finger touches the tip of the thumb; the other fingers are straight. The breath is relaxed and there is no eye focus indicated. Feel the essence of a saintly, enlightened being, such as Buddha. Graciously be a supreme being, surveying your entire surroundings. **11 minutes.**

2. Extend the arms parallel to the ground, and make a cup of the hands. The pinkie side of the hands come together. Feel the entire cosmos come through your hands to the center of the spine and down into the earth. **2 minutes.**

Comments: This meditation will help you to connect with the vastness and the power of consciousness.

Chapter Five

The Knowledge

To Substantiate It

Changes, transformation, and inner growth lead to new external situations. In our progress toward excellence, from our known to our unknown, we need new approaches for addressing the challenges related to these new situations. After projecting our intent, being sincere and consistent with who we are, and perceiving with humility the support of the universe, we are now called to give substance to our intent and depth to ourselves through knowledge. The vision, kept alive by courage and grit and sublimated by humility, is now in need of concrete facts, proficiency, and professionalism to progress toward completion.

Our culture refers to knowledge as being the result of a notional study of a topic, a learning process gained in school or university, or the result of firsthand life experiences. In the yogic approach, however, knowledge means learning through intuition and applying what is learned over time. If access to knowledge were gained only through the time needed to learn, we would have to take breaks and study in order to create a knowledge that we could then apply. In fact, there are two, mutually reinforcing areas that we can explore to obtain the knowledge necessary in all circumstances. The first area, which deals with perception and intuition, directly allows us to know reality, as well as the most suitable way to approach it. The second deals with our creative and analytical intelligence; with our clarity of consciousness, it is able to find, from the experiences throughout our lives up to the present, the knowledge required to excel in the new.

Think about it: When there were no books, how did the Gnostics of the past, on whose wisdom our studies are still based, acquire their knowledge? They learned from direct experience, from cornerstones of vital balances handed down from father to son, and mother to daughter. But, above all, they had developed the sensory capacity to relate to an object, a situation, a living being by listening to each of those items unconditionally. They allowed themselves to feel, in a neutral and true way, the experience that was happening to them, interpreting it without bias, and instantly knowing what to focus their awareness on. I relate, I feel, I deduce, I know—there is no need for assumptions, information, and comparisons. The intellectual work takes over later, when we catalog, memorize, and process an answer in order to replicate the experience and be able to share it. Nothing could be more innocent and perfect. It is clear that we may intuitively know how to produce heat or bring light, but we will need several attempts before we succeed in lighting a fire or building a lightbulb. This practical and intellectual process develops the know-how that will complete the work.

In addition, sometimes when we share our own perception, we spur others to apply their intelligence and their set of skills to further our knowledge and help us arrive at the final realization. We all know that having intuition does not mean that it will then be projected and implemented. However, when our attention and our commitment rest on a visible or invisible object, we can understand its nature and purpose and therefore know it.

These days, with information just a click away, we often fail to use our innate ability to know something. In time, we gradually lose the sensitivity needed to make this innate ability flow. It is true that nothing is easy and that everything requires diligence, commitment, and time. But everything is possible if our mind believes it and if awareness supports it to final achievement. As complex as a new situation can be, the problem it brings with it is always in proportion to the capacities and resources we have, even if the final achievement requires additional knowledge.

Although we may not be aware of this, we are living the lives we have prepared ourselves to live in the present moment. If we recognize this, our mind will search for different experiential information in different files located in time, and our awareness will then orchestrate the different skills of different brain areas and share the memories and their processing. If we were to look at our past experiences and find all the connections between them, we would be able to build an information network that fits perfectly with our new situations. If each neuronal association could operate the same way in which it creates habits and repetitive patterns, it could re-create a map that captures every experience useful for the knowledge we need, similar to the way a search program locates files on the computer based on the keyword used to launch the search. We may not necessarily know we have this information in our "back-up" memory, and usually the information of certain experiences taken individually does not represent a wealth of specific knowledge. However, by gathering diverse data from our past and threading it together like beads on a mala, we can create a sutra that will contain the necessary knowledge to continue. When we then connect our own mental software to search engines on a network and access others' information and experiences, we can exponentially increase the data we have, and our knowledge storehouse will rapidly build.

When our mind and our consciousness join a common network, the signal stretches past planet earth and reaches the entire universe, beyond time and space. Whether we draw from personal experiences or from the experiences of the entire universe, it is important that we move toward the correct experience. To receive the information we need, we must ask the right question and in the right way. The moment we ask the right question, we will receive a stream of information from all directions that will fill the shortage we want filled. The right question will create an empty space within us that, by universal laws, will promptly be filled by the right content. But to be able to ask the right question, our being must converge toward a single primary intention, it must recognize itself in one need—that is, the thirst to know what is necessary to serve our mission. The question will not only be the best we are able to process, but it will also be filled with the vibrational frequency that communicates our intent. When we ask the right question, knowledge will be revealed, and, with time, this flow will become constant. In time, our being and our vibration will no longer need to ask questions—we will simply receive answers. We are the answer.

The practice of Kundalini Yoga makes this process ever more evident. Very often, during my sadhana, when I am about to do a seminar, or when I am struggling with problems to solve, I get all the information concerning the priority of the moment in a constant current that I cannot contain. I have tried to write it down, but the flow is too fast. I have tried to record it, but using my voice on top of my internal voice makes me lose whole parts of what it is trying communicate. Lately I have repeatedly experienced that the current of information always reemerges in my consciousness at the right time, like seeds that, after having been planted, sprout with a little water and a ray of sun. So instead of trying to understand or memorize it, I've been letting everything happen by simply absorbing this flow of information and the associated feelings, as if they were the fruit of my experience.

Other times, while teaching, I realize that a good percentage of what I say has been unknown to me until I hear my own voice saying it. This natural phenomenon happens when we connect to a stream of consciousness that, in Kundalini Yoga, we call the Golden Chain. It moves and lives in the universe, enriched by the energy of masters, teachers, and practitioners of all times. To connect to this stream, we need not only the intention, but also mental silence, the ability to listen, to attend to the projection and expansion of the flow itself. Honesty and our own priorities are the two coordinates needed to access and tap into the flow of teachings or into any flow of consciousness. Once again: I relate, I feel, I deduce, I know.

This book represents an example of what I have been describing. I have never had great talent as a writer, and putting my thoughts on paper doesn't happen easily; it requires a lot of time and energy. I wrote my first book in 2000, and soon after, I wrote two others, edited and published by a dear friend whom I respect a great deal and who sought every possible way to dissuade me from continuing to write. I did not listen to her, but I did put many of her suggestions into practice. I started by writing instructional and technical books, dedicated to a public that was already practicing Kundalini Yoga. In my third book, however, I began to share the teachings with a wider audience. This latest book represents a new challenge for me in that it isn't structured in a didactic way; instead, it shows the key points of our Master's teachings, using, as a practical example, my own experience.

As I write about this journey through the Eight Elements of Excellence, sharing with you my deepest personal details, I have become increasingly aware of how I have been imbued with the teachings. I am writing the opposite of how I've always written in the past. The knowledge necessary to write this book comes to me as I am writing it, even if what I am writing about is my life, which, at first glance, may not seem the best example of the Eight Elements. When I reread a chapter, confirmations and verifications of what I have written suddenly manifest themselves. Looking back at my life through the lens of awareness, the intuition with which I have explored the presence of the Eight Elements of Excellence given by Yogi Bhajan is revealed time after time, with clearness and precision. This gives me a feeling of completeness, even though I recognize that my contribution is limited to the time devoted to the honor of writing

I now recognize that in the past—in whatever I did, for better or for worse—I always knew about the reasons that pushed me to act or to flee, the states of mind that moved me, and the holes I was trying to fill. Now I use this awareness to help me have more experience and knowledge. Although in the past, I did not always respond to this awareness for the better, I got to know my dark, hidden areas, which I have since taken care of through yoga. In fact, being rebellious, restless, and fickle probably allowed me more experience and knowledge than if I had been the good boy everyone saw and wanted.

Let me share with you a technique that has gradually taken shape over time; I call it throwing a stone across the river. Once I have set an intention, I feel the responsibility to sustain and nourish it with the projection—devoting care, attention, time, and energy to it. I imagine throwing this intention ahead of me, like throwing a stone across a river, and then I commit to go and get the stone. My responsibility to this intention is like a golden thread, binding me to it. I wait until my fears, my desires, and my rationality make me resist less, and then I follow the golden thread—like a game of tug of war between my heart and the intention—to where the stone has landed. In this way, I have reached almost everything I have set my intention on—so, I know it works. Our ego plays many games: the game of attachment, of not feeling ready, of fearing failure or loss of what we already have. In these games, if we throw our heart over the obstacles put up by our egos, it helps pull everything else across. All imaginary disabilities dissolve, and knowledge wells up through our commitment to crossing that river. In fact, by throwing the stone, an extension of us has already crossed the river. If, however, we wait to come out from undercover, until we have knowledge or until we are at our best, we risk wasting our lives in waiting. If we try to prepare, we will be ready tomorrow for what we needed today, and tomorrow, the knowledge that we gained today will already be obsolete. In fact, the same pressure we felt yesterday in not feeling ready, we will experience today, because we are ready, but only for what was required yesterday.

In Yogi Bhajan's words, *"Never say I don't know"* and *"When the time is on you, start and the pressure will be off."* [11] We are the lock, and we are the key. We have the solution for each block and the knowledge for each feeling of ignorance; for each fear, we have equal amounts of love. We are what we allow ourselves to be, and we know what we allow ourselves to know. If even the spermatozoon has the innate ability, intelligence, and knowledge to move, fight, find, circle, penetrate, and conquer to become part of a whole and be, why do we imagine we can't do the same? Do we think the spermatozoon has an easy life, or that he asks himself whether he will fail or lose his life in the race against thousands of his peers to conquer a fertile egg? Our life contains all the perfect situations, people, and dynamics that, over time, will generate the experiences we need to gain the knowledge necessary for us to seize all available opportunities.

As an example of knowledge gleaned from past experiences, we have seen what our parents' levels of security, determination, sovereignty, and perseverance can evoke in us. Suppose, in a conflictual relationship, your parents were insecure, depressed, mediocre, and erratic. That wouldn't mean that you gained less knowledge from them, and neither is the experience worse for you. However, if your mind catalogs their actions as wrong or unjust, then your knowledge and experience may be less. This doesn't mean you won't be able to reach excellence. In reality, we perfectly know the opposite polarity to bring to light; we know its pain, its dynamics. We can easily understand that the experience is of equal value and that the opportunity to reach the mountaintop is far more adventurous than already being on top. Just as poverty is the beginning of the process toward wealth, our apparent shortages are launch pads toward excellence.

I had an amazing father, a self-made man. He escaped from an irresponsible father and began working early on to pursue his dreams and realize them. He was appreciated and well-liked, and he loved being so. He was proud of himself and believed only in himself. He always took what he wanted by force. Very magnetic and a hard worker, he always seemed to be crossed by an underground stream of anger that welled up when things didn't follow his plans. I loved and feared him at the same time. He was physically strong, mentally tough, intuitive in business, impulsive in love affairs. He loved life and was a successful man of the Age of Pisces. He moved with little connection to the flow of the universe and with little awareness of others, though he knew people very well and how they could serve his cause. In me, he at first saw the handsome son, and he was proud of this. As a child, I spent a lot of time with him—he would often take me to events and trips, and I studied him, mesmerized by his exuberance.

As I grew up, however, I began to discover that my personality contrasted his, and I began to criticize and oppose his way of seeing things and the way he related to me. In times of academic failure, I would offer him my time, at his disposal, so that I could learn from him, but he would turn to me with no respect. In my few attempts at talking to him, I allowed him to flatten my self-esteem. He would often say that I did not have his strength, and, believing his words, I would flee, I would not commit, and I would feel weak. All of this aroused in him dangerous bouts of anger. After suffering the effects of his fits of rage a couple times, I decided it was healthier for me to get away, to the point of trying to escape from home, but with little success. After my parents divorced, my mother would tell him about my adolescent crises, and to him, they were more of a problem than a chance to educate me. This deteriorated our relationship even further.

In my early twenties, after being away from my father for more than three years, with no connection at all, his girlfriend called me, and I agreed to meet him. He had discovered he was suffering from a serious illness, with symptoms that were already emerging and would only get worse. I began looking after him. The disease progressed more and more, and he spoke and moved with difficulty. His girlfriend, unable to handle the situation, left after a while, and I moved into his house with the woman I was going to marry. We all lived together, working and going through crises of all kinds. I served him like one serves a teacher, and I honored him as I could.

In time, a curious mechanism established itself: I had become an extension of this stubborn man, this former sportsman who was still very angry, who could not move and act the way he wanted. However, I was an extension that differed from his vision, principles, and values. Perhaps because he was unable to fight back, or maybe because he liked the feeling of being able to move through me and into situations that were new to him, he gradually began to accept what I was doing, even when I began to move away from our common base of teaching at the gym to explore other work.

In the past, by refusing his example, I ended up falling into his mistakes. Now I could finally stop feeling inappropriate, and I could expose myself to life. The stories of my travels, my adventures, my successes, my climbing and skiing, my own ideas were, to him, an eye on a world in which he could no longer participate. All this nurtured him and made him proud of me. During his illness, my father would write me letters that, going forward in time, contained fewer and fewer warnings and criticism and more and more unconditional support and incentives to continue living my life. His strength emerged not to be shown but to be given. He understood that he had a man in front of him, even if this man differed from his vision of what a son should be.

During the last days of his life, I would leave home in the morning asking him not to die before I returned. Two nights before he left us, I was able to sit him up and ask him to fix our relationship once and forever. I told him that whatever had happened between us—any misunderstanding, remorse, or regret—was to be forgiven, unconditionally and immediately. Unable to speak, he made signs with his eyes and nodded his head. We wept together, like two prisoners who had just been released, one nearing the end of his life and the other at the beginning. When the time came, I held his hand like you hold the hand of someone who is hanging off a cliff. This man, though now placid (to use his word), was like an old tiger that roars with his mouth closed because he still wants to live. I talked to him to help him let go and to facilitate his passing—like I will do for myself. We did it together, but his heart, stronger than mine, continued to beat during the last, interminable absence of oxygen. He went as he had lived, fighting.

That time when I was alone with my father, as he was leaving his physical body, was a kind of suspended animation. No one called or visited. Afterward, I was calmer and more lucid than ever before. I consoled my mother and left. When I saw my son, I looked at him with different eyes; I realized then the impact that I had on his life and the knowledge that he would inherit through me. He was crying, but I told him how I was honored to have witnessed his grandfather's last breath and that there was no reason to be afraid. The basic knowledge that I carry with me now is not the part of my father that lives in me, but the experience of our relationship, the result of a conscious interaction with him as a father, as a man, as an archetype.

My Master, whom I had met about five years before my father's death, was the same age as my father. My Master's teachings guided my relationship with my father toward excellence. If I had not come across the teachings, I would not have been able to complete the experience with love, thus enriching my knowledge. In the relationship with my father, despite starting out with a lack of elevating elements, we were able to play the divine game that, in the yogic tradition, is known as *Ape Guru Chela,* in which the teacher becomes the student and the student becomes the teacher. Anyone can offer us the opportunity to learn, even from their mistakes. Knowledge is everywhere—most of all, in ourselves. It wells up when we take the risk of staying in our fear until we discover it to be nonexistent; when we dare not depend on other human beings, but only on God that dwells in us; when we stop caring about surviving and realize that everything is just waiting to flow toward us; when we realize that we have no other way to achieve ourselves than to light our spirit and be so happy we become a lighthouse in other peoples' lives. We may have to suffer for this, but the experience gained will be the knowledge that gives substance to our action, complete and perfect, toward excellence.

Sarab Gyan Kriya

April 2, 2001

Posture: Sit straight in a cross-legged position.

Mudra: Both hands are in Gyan Mudra. Rest the right hand in the left in front of the Heart Center, so that the tips of the mudra in each hand come together, the thumbs and index fingers are touching, palms facing up. Elbows are relaxed down.

Eyes: Closed.

Mantra: Ek Ong Kaar Sat Gur Prasaad, Sat Gur Prasaad Ek Ong Kaar. Chant aloud. Ek Ong Kar Satgur Prasad by Nirinjan Kaur was used in the original class.

Time: 31 minutes.

To end: Inhale deeply, suspend the breath and extend the arms straight up with the palms together. Like a salute, the body will distribute the energy through neutral channels. Exhale. Inhale deeply, suspend the breath and exhale. Inhale deeply, press the hands together and synchronize the body from toe to top. Relax.

Comments: As one obtains true happiness, intercommunication evolves from sexual to sensual, social, local, national, international and cosmic to the Infinite. Out of that, Prakirti, the universe, is born. The mantra, *Ek Ong Kaar Sat Gur Prasaad, Sat Gur Prasaad Ek Ong Kaar* explains it and this most sacred kriya is the seal to go with it. The mudra by itself will change the flow of your body's energy. Do this kriya, make it part of your life, and you will be surprised at the changes in you.

Chapter Six

The Prayer

To Feed It

To excel is to go beyond our own limits, surpass our apparent self, and manifest the radiance of our own essence. Excelling over others is only a consequence; it is not the motivation that should move us to excel. The proof of our excellence lies not in being better than others, which is an attempt to convince ourselves of our own value, thus avoiding personal insecurity. The test rather consists in being able to excel over ourselves by winning our subconscious dynamics, transcending our fears, and rising beyond our imaginary disabilities. We excel not to stand out from other human beings (as in ex-cellere or pre-cellere in Latin), but to be more like the Greek concept of kassandros, where kad is "to excel" and andros means "man": the man who excels in himself and for himself.

Without excellence, we remain confused in the mediocrity of the crowd, because we are confused in ourselves. We identify with our personalities, neuroses, and paradigms, unaware of our true potential and our true essence. To move toward excellence, we must explore our unknown and find out what there is of ourselves beyond what we allow ourselves to accept as possible. The medium that allows us to relate to our unknown and push past the known boundaries we have established is prayer.

Prayer is not an attempt to establish communication with our soul, because our soul is always with us. It's not even talking to God, for He listens to everything, always. Prayer is accessing our unknown self to awaken the God inside us from His sleep. Far from being purely religious, prayer is the human being's most powerful and basic power—and it's powerful! Prayer nourishes the intention of achieving our vision, and it raises and maintains the skills necessary to excel.

> Prayer is tapping energy from my own Unknown. Whenever you want to reach your own Unknown, you pray. And the only channel through which your own Unknown can reach you for help is the power of your own prayer. Prayer is not talking to God.[12]

On our journey toward excellence, prayer is, in my opinion, the most tangible and identifiable of the Eight Elements. Every achievement of something that seemed unlikely, each change of gear and direction, any stream of prosperity that poured into my life was a response to something I had projected unconsciously or with a clear intention.

Born and raised in Rome—a city associated for centuries with being one of the world's leading seats of religion, a city that houses the very core of the Catholic church—and educated in Catholic schools and environments, I have always had prayer as part of my life. And yet, whenever I brought my palms together during mass, before going to sleep, or before a meal, my attitude was mostly ritualistic and mechanical. Only rarely would I sense a true connection. My understanding of prayer then was far from what I am able to perceive now as a prayer.

Every action, word, or thought can move and dwell in a state of prayer. Prayer is a sacred and neutral space. It is unaffected by the seeds of doubt and duality. It can connect us to our infinite unknown, so we can access our resources and true potential, provide for our needs, be supported on our path, or simply dwell in a state of gratitude. In the Western world, we have been taught to pray to someone or something outside of us, bigger and better, someone who can work a miracle to resolve or change the events in our lives. We have created the conditions for believing that God is outside of us. But believing in an external force that makes things happen separates us from the generating power.

Many of us have old understandings of prayer. We imagine sitting and begging a distant deity or saint for acknowledgment or to fill a need. In this way we were taught to wish, ask, and plead rather than communicate heart to heart, recognize our Infinite and confirm our consciousness. The Aquarian approach is different. We feel no separation between the Infinite, God, and our Self. That means the task of prayer is understood in a new way. To understand and apply this Aquarian perspective, we may have to recognize our old images of prayer and adjust them to learn it in this new way. Another wrong concept is that you are a sinner, and you must redeem yourself. If I am made in the image of God, what is my sin? How can the image be sin? And what way can sin be in me? I am very sinful when my Unknown is not with me. I am weak, I am feeble, and I go through temptation. I try to do things which have no concept, reality, or reaction. I just want to get away with things: I play politics with myself. I can juggle things with myself, and that's all I have been doing with myself. But that does not mean that I'm sinning. Simply, when I am not connected with my Unknown, and I do not tap my own power of the Unknown, at that time, I am weak. My weakness is not from somebody else making me weak. That is not true. Nobody can make me strong, and nobody can make me weak. I make myself strong, and I make myself weak. When I connect to my Unknown with my own prayer, I am very strong. And when I am not connected, I am very weak. It's that simple. I know you cannot believe it, because you have been told something different all these years. Well, you believed that, now just try to believe this. What you believed before didn't work. If you believe this, it will work. [13]

If we are following logic and knowledge and something we were expecting doesn't happen or, on the contrary, something unexpected happens, we call it a miracle. But we are the ones who create the condition to believe in miracles. Yoga teaches us that when we include a prejudice or preconception in our dynamic interpretation of reality, we remain in our limitations and live and progress as planned. But by practicing yoga to increase our level of perception and tolerance toward events, we allow ourselves to relate to reality by remaining spontaneous and original, without necessarily trying to confirm, through our behavior, our paradigms. If we can remove that feeling of separation from the generating force, we can open ourselves to the possibility of perceiving that same power within us. It is not about believing; rather it is about feeling freely, without feeling separated from situations to which we relate and from events that happen to us. As the saying goes, *"If you meet Buddha, kill him"* (a koan attributed to Zen Master Linji). If we meet Buddha in front of us, then we are still in a state of duality, separate. We must kill the vision we have created of a separate Buddha and keep practicing until Buddha is within us. In other words, we must not believe the representation of our preconceptions, not even if we see it right in front of us.

Prayer is innate in human beings and inherent in our nature, but like any other faculty, it has to be cultivated, experienced, and understood. Our prayers must not be directed at something outside and separate from us; instead, they should be directed toward the unknown within us, which is simply a place that has yet to be explored. So, is praying simply reduced to talking to ourselves? In a way, yes. But our life will blossom and prosper in proportion to the depth and innocence with which we pray.

It took me a whole year to understand the impact, the orbit, and the effects of prayer. Yogi Bhajan tells us that thirty-six years of age is when the second Cycle of Life Energy begins, a cycle that changes every eighteen years and during which time we review the overall quality of our life. During major phase transitions, we feel like part of us is dying, but this death makes way for a new world. After five or six years of intense yogic practice, I entered a deep crisis at age thirty-six. I felt a sense of separation from the generating power and from my true self during my practice of deep meditation with the mantra, *"Aad Sach Jugaad Sach Hai Bhee Sach Nanak Hosee Bhee Sach:* "True in the Beginning, True throughout the Ages, True Here and Now, Nanak says, forever shall be True"[†] My awareness was merging into the meditation and perceiving its effects in every area. As I progressed in my daily practice, I noticed that the scale and magnitude of the meditation were too big for me to contain at that given moment. There were still too many patterns and too much dirt in my subconscious, still too little tolerance in my nervous system to contain the experience, and still a too strong ego, which required temporary gratification through known things. In response, my ego began a full-fledged revolt, nagging like a whimsical child, strategic like a stubborn and sneaky adult. Several aspects of my life started being undermined—in particular, my relationships and my self-confidence. My prayers, until then so fervent and full of demands, suffered a stall. I was tempted to make the conditions being dictated by my ego the objects of my prayers. I was also embarrassed to admit that I didn't know whether I should pray to receive the awareness necessary to overcome the crisis, which, though it made me suffer, also attracted me. So I prayed for the one thing that I knew I could not risk losing—my daily yoga practice. Like a boat clinging to its anchor in stormy seas, I knew my sadhana would carry me through the eye of the storm.

† This mantra by Guru Nanak Dev Ji is part of the Mul Mantra, which is at the very beginning of Japji Sahib. As per Yogi Bhajan's teachings, this mantra connects a person to the infinite.

During this time, my progress toward excellence began to falter, and the main relationships in my life, especially the one with my partner, who then became the mother of my second child, started getting caught up in the inner conflict, the intolerance, and the sense of separation that I was feeling. On one hand, I felt like I was denying my instinctive side, that I was crying out for attention; on the other, I felt like I was lacking consistency and commitment to my higher Self and to the teachings. I felt guilty and rebellious at the same time.

This process, which started in autumn, a season that has always given me the urge to move and revise the orbit of my life, dragged on and reached its peak in summer. By that time, I was mentally exhausted by the enormous amount of assumptions, ideas, and thoughts that I had put under consideration for the resolution of my problem, though I was well aware that it could not be resolved through a purely intellectual process. If only I had acted from my awareness, everything would have found its own context and would have transformed from problems into considerations, into emotional movements; I would have seen that it was just the old resisting the new. However, I didn't want to know about the possibility of such a shift. The idea of leaving that suffering and not being able to satisfy the ego's needs anymore seemed to me more like dying than being free. Praying for awareness, and risking, or rather knowing for sure, that awareness would come, was out of the question.

Like any person won over by his own ego, I became a hypocrite. I learned to hide behind mediocrity, which is where human beings take refuge when they refuse to stand up to their responsibilities and their radiance. I had no choice but to return again, a recidivist, to the presence of my Master, to let him slam the truth in my face, to hear him say what I already knew, and mostly, to ask him for a little love, something I felt I was missing because I thought it could only be found on the outside. And, judging by my ego's hunger, I would never have enough love to satiate me.

I spent a month in the United States and attended all of Yogi Bhajan's workshops. However, my every attempt to meet him in person, whether upon his arrival, during breaks, or before he left the venue, gave no result. My Master didn't look at me, not even when I found myself in front of him, and when I finally did manage eye-to-eye contact, he looked at me with such disregard that he made me feel even worse. Finally, I had the opportunity to formally request a private meeting with him, and his assistant assured me that she would get me an appointment in person. But when I later asked her for confirmation, she told me that it was impossible because of too many consultations and too little time. I felt, on one hand, a sense of relief, but on the other, deep despair. I convinced some friends to invite him over for dinner and managed to receive just a little wink from him. He was screaming, pretending to be angry with a couple. When the couple, unable to hold his gaze, bowed their heads, he saw me behind them. His face went from irate to smiling, and his eyes met mine like a spark. That was it, nothing else. My last day in the United States, at the end of July, I missed my return flight so I could write him a letter.

Upon my return to Italy, things around me were unchanged, though I was a bit softer and could handle the conflict a little better. Still jetlagged, I went to the beach to play in the water with my eldest son and my nephews. While out in the surf, a crack, audible even from under water, signaled that my right knee had broken. My son took me out of the water, and I knew right away, from the pain and knee position, that I had broken the meniscus, and that its fragments were blocking the joint. Internally furious, but externally calm, I found that I could handle the pain if I stood still and kept the knee bent. My first lucid thought was that the knee, corresponding to the navel point, represents pride and ego. When you bring your knees to the ground, you become humble and prayerful, and I realized I could no longer do that. The knee determines direction and movement, and someone had finally stopped me. I couldn't move, I couldn't do, and I couldn't be. I reviewed every place my knee had taken me in the past eight months—where I had stood, where I had faltered. I understood and accepted that God had orchestrated characters, environment, and time in perfect sync. Once home, everyone offered suggestions about what to do: hospitals, X-rays, MRIs, surgery. Some people tried to touch my knee, but I would not allow it. When they finally persuaded me to go to the hospital, I refused to be examined by the doctor. Back home, while everyone urged me to seek medical advice, I realized that I would not be able to practice yoga as I had been, but I reassured myself by thinking of possible alternatives to maintain my practice. Within, I prayed and felt grateful. To all people present, I declared, "God broke my knee, and God will put it right." I said it loud and daring, and, although I believed it, I felt a chill run down my spine: I was either truly connected or completely insane. The phone rang and a student told me about another student's father who specialized in knee operations. I was given an appointment, and, three days after the accident, this was the first doctor I trusted to carry out the operation on my knee.

Fall came round again, and my knee was still swollen and needed syringing. Having started to teach right after the operation, my knee troubles continued. And yet the accident had made me humbler, softer, and calmer. My meditative practice was good, and my motivation came back to being clear and nurturing of my prayers. I was the author of everything, and I was in constant interaction with my unknown. When I had gone to see my Master during my crisis, instead of helping me alleviate my troubles, he had instead shown the excellence to increase the pressure so I could go through the process and come out on the other side. Now my crisis had scaled down to only a few thoughts here and there, though I was still a little in need of love. But even so, my anchor was solid, and the compass was pointing in the right direction.

One day in October, my partner told me I had received a letter. I realized that my heart had felt like it had been in the trenches, waiting for a letter from his beloved, a thousand miles away. I asked if it was from Yogi Bhajan. She nodded. Athough my heart felt full, I was contained as I sat down to read. But after the first three words, "I love you," I could not contain myself anymore; along with the joy, I released all I had held inside me—the physical pain, the stress of the last years spent in doubt, my father's death four months earlier. My Master had waited for the exact moment when I was out of the crisis, the moment when I could find in myself the ability to transcend and make the decision to move forward. It would have been much easier for him to provoke me during my crisis, rather than handling me by letting me go. I also understood that the love I was looking for outside, even within the relationship with my partner, could not match the unconditional love a Master can give with the sole intent of making the student ten times better than himself.

I cannot say more. What I felt cannot be explained with words; it can only be understood by experiencing it. I understood that a Master lives in a state of prayer and that his words and decisions are in the flow of prayer. That year's crisis was a blessing, an answer to my prayer to grow in awareness, but I was not able to recognize it as such until I had surrendered. I'd had to find my balance on one leg, slow down, and get help.

We pray to defend ourselves against non-sense and make sense out of it. There is nothing outside, and what happens is not important; what is important is how we react. *Aad Sach Jugaad Sach Hai Bhee Sach Nanak Hosee Bhee Sach*: "True in the Primal Beginning, True throughout the Ages, True Here and Now. Nanak says, forever shall be True." The only thing that is real and that exists is the self. Anything else exists only in proportion to how much the self allows us to get in touch with and be influenced by. How the self acts and reacts to the event is far more important than the event itself. We pray to get to know our own self, to be able to serve it and express it, to relate directly to events. Only then can we pray for the well-being and prosperity of others. To pray, we must be clear in our intent.

Prayer forces us to truth and priorities. Prayer must be projected with neutrality and strength. We also must be able to recognize the answer when and where it arrives. If there is coherence among the conscious, the subconscious, and the intention we project, then the answer is guaranteed. It is not necessary to make a request, but just to be in a state of gratitude. Being desperate makes the prayer precise and effective. Love makes it foolproof. Surrendering to the flow of life, to the will of the universe, turns a human being into a living prayer.

Meditation to Teach You to Pray

March 29, 1996

Mudra: Interlace your fingers so the left Mercury finger (pinky finger) is on the outside. Extend your Jupiter fingers (index fingers) up straight. Cross the thumb, so the right is over the left. Place this mudra in front of your Heart Center; the thumbs are very close to the chest, and the Jupiter fingers are pointing straight up toward the ceiling.

Eyes: Closed or 1/10th open.

Mental Focus: Build an image of yourself. You are still and radiant. Your breath is slow, deep and meditative. Imagine you are sitting on the top of Mt. Everest, so all the world is around you. Consider your spine is like a tube of light. There is light between the base of your neck and the base where you are sitting. Now it is sending out light rays. You can send waves to the entire globe with each thought. Your prayer is like a stone, which is dropped in the middle of some water. It creates waves and ripples. Feel yourself as the waves and ripples go on and on unto Infinity. The power of your soul is the pure power. Let the power of your soul vibrate out. It has no limit or boundary. With each breath and with the ripples of your heartbeat project, bless and be blessed. Merge in Infinity and let Infinity find you, too.

Time: 11 minutes to a maximum of 31 minutes.

To End: Holding the position, begin a heavy Breath of Fire to awaken yourself out of the meditation. Continue for 1 minute. Then stretch your arms out to the sides at about a 45-degree angle, palms down. Begin circling just your hands, right hand counterclockwise and left hand clockwise. Stop every so often as the hands are up and out to the sides, and flutter your fingers a little; as if you are sending off energy to the environment and space around you.

Chapter Seven

The Grace

To Carry Yourself Through It

Some people have such an amazing and impressive impact on society and on the environment that they are remembered for generations. Among these, however, rare are the ones who make history for having honored and served others and for having elevated the awareness of an era or a generation. More common are those who have abused and exploited others in favor of their own authority and personal well-being. These characters are extraordinarily capable of reaching their goal. Their prerogative is to take care of every single aspect of the process, with the obscure charisma shown by those who know what to do and have the tools to do it. In our day, especially in politics, there are people so capable that we can't help but ask ourselves what they would be able to achieve if only their capabilities were aimed toward a common goal, a common prosperity, used for a good cause.

Some people have reversed the course of history, making possible what, until then, had not even been imaginable, sometimes giving life to something only a disturbed and vindictive mind could conjure. There is no doubt that in order to convince people to follow them, to support them in their cause, to combat and defeat those who opposed them, they had vision, courage, and determination. They might have felt guided by a higher power; they may have had knowledge derived from study, observation, and experience; and they may have even prayed to their God or their devil. And yet the way they did all this—beyond the objective they had set themselves, elevated or not—relegated them to the shadows of darkness, and their success was temporary rather than permanent, personal, and shared. Even those who start out with the best intentions, the highest purposes, and visions of a collective welfare can end up failing in the way they pursue the goal, especially if they get caught up in the ego's boundaries.

Grace is the substantial difference with which we deliver ourselves, interact with others, and relate to the Infinite. Victory without grace is a result gained through manipulation; it's a shout of joy with no sound; it is lost in mediocrity. Without grace, you can temporarily win over someone, but you inevitably lose against yourself. If you are in a state of grace, however, you are moved by a pure and fearless intent, you have nothing to gain and nothing to lose. You move beyond the pros and cons, and you feel and act in a neutral and intuitive way, uninfluenced by negative opposition or positive support. You are fully involved, yet unattached to the result. Perfectly on time, you are in sync with the flow of life, and you experience the real Infinite in yourself and in others, because you are beyond the concept of gain and loss. You are free and vast, unassailable and incorruptible.

The difference between excelling and exceeding is given by how we proceed, love, fight, negotiate, live, or die. Either we move out of our ego or we exceed in our ego. With grace, we move out of our ego and elevate ourselves and others. Seeking success or excellence without grace can only lead to an ego outburst. To be graceful, we need to go beyond our self, our needs, and our impulsivity; we must find within ourselves the assurance of being complete in ourselves, with no other desire than to serve and honor.

My Master's entire life was based on and lived with grace. In particular, he gave me two examples of his grace that I would like to share with you. At the beginning of the relationship with my partner, who later became the mother of my second child, we went through a particularly intense crisis. We tried to deal with it using yogic tools and finally decided to sit at the feet of the Master, where we had first met, and expose ourselves to him to identify the problem that was, frankly, eluding us. We were at the European Yoga Festival in France, and Yogi Bhajan received us in his room, which was full of people. He listened for a while and then began to poke and provoke my partner to a crescendo. At first, this lifted me from feeling at fault, but after a while, it just seemed too much. He never spoke directly to me. Only at the end, when he was explaining the ways in which we would have to relate to each other, did he turn to us both. Stunned—me more than her—we tried to put the pieces of the experience together. However, what started in that room was more an internal process than guidelines for the future or laying the blame on either one of us. It took me months to realize that Yogi Bhajan had turned to my companion, putting her under pressure, only because she was able to contain his impact. In reality, 70 percent of what he had said was aimed at me, but I had been unable to receive it at the time. As much as I could, I have treasured that experience.

After our meeting, I began to review myself and relate to my partner and to life with a different attitude. But the consequences of doing so brought me to the crisis I shared with you in the previous chapter. During the summer I spent in the United States at my Master's feet, he had treated me as if I did not exist. At the end of class one day, I tried to relate to him. We had just ended a long and beautiful meditation that had evidently given me a bit of courage and boldness. People began raising their hands to ask questions. Most of the questions were not very relevant or intelligent: For example, a woman asked Yogi Bhajan if he believed in ghosts and forest goblins. I thought he would rise and throw the small wooden table he had beside him. But, instead, calm and smiling, he began his answer saying, "Darling . . .". I don't recall exactly what else he said, but I remember being shocked and surprised by his gentle manner. Exhausted by his indifference toward me and depressed by not receiving his help, I stood and raised my hand. Yogi Bhajan stared at me so fiercely the whole room stopped breathing. He said something like, "What do you want?" I asked what the meditation we had just done was for, and, as I formulated the question, I instantly knew it was wrong. "You idiot! How dare you ask this question? You should know, you idiot. You should feel what it was for! Do you understand?" His background as an army officer was clear from the way his words thundered. It reminded me of when I was doing the compulsory military service and my terrifying battalion commander—the only difference was that I didn't believe or trust my ex-commander, but I did trust my Master. I tried to stand straight and said, "Yes, sir," but in a voice too weak for his ears, so I had to say it louder, again and again. When he became convinced that I realized how stupid I was, he gave one of the most beautiful definitions of the effects of meditation in general, which filled my blank mind. After class, I had random thoughts like,

"At least he related to me—I really am an idiot—now he believes I can contain the impact of his confrontation—he wants me to experience shame in front of everybody—why am I not allowed to ask but only to feel?"

I now recognize that all those thoughts made sense, and I see that the gears started shifting in me then. My Master, choosing between his many personalities, had dealt a precise and merciless blow, risking my misunderstanding and who knows what other consequences. He could have talked to me first, explained things, given me a practice to follow, comforted me—anything that might resemble our idea of grace. But he was sharp, bitter, and heavy. At the end, someone said he often chose a person to teach the whole class and not to take it personally. But I decided to take it at every level; I let myself be swept away by every sensation, and that was the right thing to do. He had demonstrated perfectly what it means to be impersonally personal. Here's what I found years later in his lectures:

We are going through this series on a relationship of faith. You trust me. I trust you. You come here to learn from me. God has given me the privilege to serve you. I don't play that game of, "I have got you, and you have got me." You don't get me; I don't get you. It is just a simple privilege to serve you; and it is a privilege to honor that somebody touched me and I learned it and I enjoyed it and I still recall and relish those experiences.[14]

This man had a vision and an intention, and he served it. Winning or losing were none of his business. Yet, despite this guidance and example, it still remains difficult for me to have grace.

I believe I can be a good example of a person who makes graceful choices and who maintains graceful relationships and responsibilities, and yet rarely are my manners graceful in action. This is especially evident when I am very involved in something, and the obstacles and dynamics I meet seem inconceivable to me. It's not that I haven't had examples of grace. It's not that I do not know grace's importance, that I do not understand it is the key to true excellence. It's not that my teacher didn't show me grace and that I haven't been poked and provoked to show grace. It's just that my manners often lack it. In those times when I do lose my grace, I go all the way and lose it completely, because the moment I realize I am about to lose it, I always choose to exceed, like a vice I do not want to give up, like a vicious habit of which I know the consequences but decide once again to give in to.

Any dynamic can be changed, corrected, and interrupted, but only if we decide to. Even the most ingrained habit can be removed, the most stagnant role can be abandoned, the most instinctive reaction can be avoided, if a conscious process leads us to really want it. Those aspects and tendencies of ourselves that are inconvenient to our logical awareness or that are inconsistent with our identity and role have the right to exist because we have not yet decided to be rid of them. If we look carefully, we will discover that we are both the prison guard and the one who sets us free. Yoga is a great tool, not only because it weeds out inappropriate habits and automatically plants new, elevating attitudes, but also because by practicing yoga, we can come to understand what we want and be aware of how to achieve it. It is a conscious process of knowledge of ourselves and our will; it is intended to help us express ourselves. However bold, difficult, or atypical our vision of ourselves fully manifested may be, the mind will become flexible enough to be able to see it realized. And yet, all this is only a good starting point—it may facilitate the process—but it's not enough to give us grace.

Grace cannot be captured, studied, or understood. Grace showers the human being like a wave breaking on the shore, rearranging the sand at its own will, drawing more and different textures and geometries, to which the grains of sand do not resist. The sand becomes infinitesimal parts of a puzzle that writes the sea's will on the shore. In the same way, the human being, showered by Divine flow, writes the will and the power of the Infinite with effectiveness, precision, and grace. But this cannot happen if we are motivated by personal gain or fear of loss. When we suspend every action of the ego, that is when grace manifests its wonders.

We must not confuse being graceful with not being resolved, sharp as a knife, explosive, provocative, and even manipulative. Everything is allowed in the state of grace, but our actions must never be reactive. We can *pretend* to be angry, but we cannot *be* angry. We can use every facet of our personality that we believe effective, but all without reacting. In a state of grace, we exist without the needs and constraints of the ego. Guided by a neutral stream of consciousness and not by subconscious patterns, mental intrigues, and hidden agendas, we can draw on those memories that, consistent with the situation, are uplifting and elevating.

The climber who is in the flow of grace is not afraid to fall or fail to reach the mountaintop. He is what he is doing, and he dances between the rock and the sky, playing with the limits of physical laws. The actor in a state of grace doesn't seek the approval of the public or satisfaction through the performance. He is lost in a creative flow and becomes magnetic and truer than reality. The yogi does not get distracted trying to give a name to what happens to him; he neither resists nor judges his experience: he is simply who he is and where he is. The lover doesn't ask questions, doesn't seek, compare, compete—the lover no longer poses conditions in giving his love. But how many of us are ready to become nothing so that everything may flow through us? Who is willing, at least for a moment, to lean on the brink of fear of not existing in order to exist completely? The one who accomplishes this will be showered with grace.

So, where does grace come from? Which set of attitudes and virtues makes it manifest? What state of consciousness does grace deliver? In Yogi Bhajan's words:

> *Grace is not a monopoly of the individual. Grace is the prayer of the individual . . . and this, humans have not learned. Period. Grace is the prayer. Where there is a prayer, there shall be a grace. Where there is no grace, there's no prayer. Period. Life is the gift, not the monopoly of the individual. Grace comes from perpetual prayer. You know, it's not something you can learn from me.*[15]

Prayer is the source of grace. But we pray in fits and starts, we pray to ask, we pray out of fear, we pray to keep the illusion of being separate from the creative force. We pray to stay alive, instead of living in a state of prayer. We may be able to show grace when things go as we want, but when, for our own paradigms and mind-sets, what happens is inconceivable, when something hurts us or our ego, when everything seems against us, that is the test of grace. Every time we are under pressure, every time we become anxious, the nature of our limitations is highlighted. And yet, instead of closing off or fighting or running away, every human being has the ability to be graceful:

Capacity of the man is not that he can catch God by a tail. Capacity of man is not that he can create miracles. Capacity of a man is not that he is most successful; he is beautiful; he is a multimillionaire; he is president of the whole world and the world bows to him. Capacity of a man depends on two things—two things. When it is impossible, according to that person, when it is impossible, his heart is kind, and his head is compassionate. There is nothing beyond that. Heart is kind. Kindness and compassion are the two things that guarantee your strength. There is no such thing as God. It is a gimmick if you produce it in any way; it is a reality if you dispense it in a simple way. You must be kind and compassionate when it is absolutely by all standards not possible.[16]

This is such a revolutionary concept: to be kind in our hearts and compassionate in our minds, when, by our personal standards, it seems impossible to do so. Where before there was the wall that marked the limit of our intolerance, now there is a window, open to new possibilities. Where before our nervous system jammed up and was forced to slow down, now it has the option of shifting into overdrive and moving faster, consuming less energy. The real adventure lies in seeing what's beyond the limit of intolerance. Transcending that limit is a phenomenal experience. To do this, we need the right lever: We must vibrate at the same frequency of the Infinite and flow in grace. The impact, sound, and flow of water breaking on a rock is different from that of waves breaking on a sandy shore. Rock will take a very long time to be carved and smoothed down by the sea. Part of it will become sand, and in a very long process, it will learn to let itself be run over by the sea. In the same way, man will learn to let himself be run over by the Divine.

My mother surprised us all, and probably also the karmic wheel, by making a choice that, in hindsight, I believe to be the most graceful thing I have ever seen her do. When my father's illness began, he was living with another woman. He had separated from my mother when I was nine years old, and at the time of his illness, I was eighteen. I was in the mandatory military service when his partner repeatedly asked me to reconnect and use their home as a base, seeing as I didn't have a fixed residence at the time. I accepted and only later realized how this woman, who'd found herself alone with a sick man, needed help. When I finished my military service, she gradually eclipsed herself until she finally disappeared, leaving my father with me. From rebellious and homeless, I became responsible at work and with my father. Shortly after, I decided to marry. My father was a warrior who didn't want to give in to a devastating disease, and I was his arms and legs. We argued a lot, and I fought for what I thought was right, sometimes even managing to influence him. But basically I served him and tried to contain his anger. My mother had been present and had helped us in the long process of the necessary medical appointments to diagnose the disease and, at least initially, had been very supportive. But after that my mother—and my sister—was out of the dynamic, each for her own good reason.

In the meantime, I had gotten married and had brought my wife into the house where I lived with my sick father. The situation was far from easy. My father needed a lot of attention, and taking care of him was grueling. My twenty-four-year-old self saw everything as a potential problem or a burden to carry. Very soon, because of my defensiveness, the relationship with my wife began to deteriorate. Exhausted, my wife told me she was thinking of leaving with our son because she could no longer bear the situation. I let a few days pass and then lifted the phone and called my mother for advice.

My mother's role in my father's life had always been that of a great supporter. Behind my father's success, there had always been my mother's help: She contained his enthusiasm, his distractions, and his pride. They separated when my father reached the height of his business and economic success, and even though I can understand that my mother's character and words had an effect on their splitting up, he certainly wasn't graceful in that context. Following the many quarrels, my mother, my sister, and I were forced to leave the house, while he remained. In reality, my father already had another woman ready to live with him. And yet, eleven years after my parents' separation, when I called to ask for help, my mother didn't even pause to think about it. She didn't try to negotiate; she just came home and took over my place, allowing me to go to my wife and son to try to save our relationship. She found herself in her old home with a sick, far from humble patient. She took care of him through highs and lows for another fourteen years, serving him until his last breath. As she had once helped him rise, she now helped him in his descent, even though she had been denied participation in my father's most successful years. Any other consideration or judgment about my mother's life is eclipsed by this great demonstration of grace.

Experiencing the Original You

April 7, 1993

Awakening the Law of Intelligence in the Original Self: If you are in a demanding situation where you have to come up with a solution, control your breath by inhaling 20 seconds, holding 20 seconds, and exhaling 20 seconds. The answer you need will come to you. I want to give you that depth and that strength which is yours…the original you.

—*Yogi Bhajan*

1. Sit in Easy Pose. Interlace your fingers and turn the mudra so that the palms face outward. Extend your arms straight out in front of you with no bend in the elbows. This is called Reverse Elbow Lock. Try to breathe only one breath per minute. Inhale for 20 seconds, hold for 20 seconds and exhale for 20 seconds. Continue this long, slow deep breathing for 3 minutes. If you have problems with your stomach and digestion, your elbows may hurt or be uncomfortable.

2. Keeping the same mudra with the eyes focused at the tip of the nose. Begin Cannon Breath through the mouth. Continuously inhale and exhale through the mouth with the force of Cannon Fire. 3 minutes. How much you can heal yourself now will be in direct proportion to the strength of your breath.

3. Keeping the same mudra, inhale, hold the breath and pump the navel. When you can no longer hold the breath, exhale; immediately inhale and again pump your navel. Continue at your own breath rhythm, pumping the navel vigorously. 3 minutes.

To end: Inhale, hold the breath 15 seconds, stretch your arms out as far as possible, putting pressure on the mudra. Exhale through the mouth like Cannon Fire. Repeat this sequence two more times.

4. To fully circulate the energy you have created, extend your Jupiter finger straight up and lock down the other three fingers with your thumb. Circle your hands in outward circles as fast as possible. This movement has to be so vigorous that the entire spine moves. 2-1/2 minutes. Inhale and relax.

Comments: If this set is practiced for 120 days you'll gain great vitality, personal excellence, and a new concept of what you are. It works on the celestial concept of the third layer of the human mind.

Chapter Eight

The Determination

To Achieve It

The wonder of the Eight Elements of Excellence lies in their heterogeneous nature. Courage, grit, knowledge, and determination are faculties of the earthly man who may not necessarily have a very high level of awareness, but who is grappling with the opportunities and challenges of life. Vision, prayer, humility, and grace are qualities we find in a spiritual being stretched toward the divine and waiting to sense the subtle energy to move and act, like the mantra: Gobinday Mukanday Udaaray Apaaray Hariang Kariang Nirnaamay Akaamay, "Sustainer, Liberator, Enlightener, Infinite, Destroyer, Creator, Nameless, Desireless." Of these eight attributes of God, the first four are tangible, human, pragmatic, and understandable, whereas the second four are divine, abstract, and unlimited. This is the game of the expanding awareness of the human being who meditates so that his instincts, confined between space and time, can draw from his infinite, unattached nature. He strives to live as a *spiritual being having a human experience, instead of as a human being having a spiritual experience. The divine qualities and attitudes do not belong to a god outside of us, but are inherent in us and can be expressed when our sense of separation dissolves.*

Being in a state of grace, beyond the concept of gain and loss, and yet remaining determined may seem like a paradox. But it isn't, if grace is the method and code of nobility with which we apply our determination. Indeed, without the vision and inspiration that come from tapping into the unknown, from communicating with our higher consciousness, and from surrendering to a vaster will and nonattachment, courage, grit, knowledge, and determination can become sterile and limited, used for personal and trivial purposes. Without an inspiration that transcends the ego's limits, we can only draw on courage, grit, knowledge, and determination like an animal, driven more by impulse and intuition than by awareness.

Determination is a precise act that becomes our priority and requires our commitment. Therefore, not only is it an element of the final momentum, but it is also present at every stage of the process, right from the beginning. Determination includes our commitment to clarifying, verifying, and estimating the size, value, and energy expenditure of the situation, object, or objective that we are considering. Determination is persistence, perseverance, even obstinacy. I've seen drug addicts use determination; I've seen myself use determination to quench whatever thirst I thought I had. Without grace, determination, confined in the restrictions of the ego, is a common factor of mediocrity. But at the same time, determination is the final impetus that allows us to achieve our goal, our vision.

We often confuse enthusiasm or passion for determination; but real determination comes only from unconditional love. If we are completely exhausted and hanging from the tiniest handhold, the desperation of the abyss below us is not enough to make sure we won't let go. We need a vaster motivation that goes beyond us and our own lives. It might be creating a precedent that can inspire others; it might be saving someone's life or completing an action designed in cooperation with the Infinite to bring a change that only we, in that time and space, can enact. Determination is recognizing that we have a specific purpose in the balance of things and then honoring that purpose with gratitude and achieving it at any cost. Any motivation below this makes determination momentary and questionable.

In truth, not being determined to achieve something is equivalent to being determined not to show determination. A lack of determination may result from a lack of self-esteem or from insecurity caused by denying oneself. If we can't love ourselves, we inevitably can't love others. Both living in indecisiveness and denying ourselves the opportunity to express ourselves fully help build the barriers that prevent us from taking the path toward excellence.

We are satisfied to have a nice house and nice car. All this is just earth bound! So long as we are not heaven bound, we have not accepted heaven. So long as we are in denial of heaven, we will be unhappy. We have come from the heavens, we are to create heavens, and we must return to the heavens. The majority of the time you are in self-denial. When you go to an interview, you prepare yourself to project well. You only want to look your best when you have

> *an opportunity to relate to! In reality, you are the opportunity! There is no other opportunity! You live in denial. You are afraid to walk tall and be gracious, open and loving. You judge everything, first in terms of commotion and emotions, second by maya and money. Third you do not want what makes you desirable; you want what fulfills your desires! In this way, life is a progressive tragedy.[17]*

The point from which we act and think and the engine that triggers our motivation both need to be reconsidered. We must move the source of our intentions from the radius of our ego's needs to the virtues of living in the excellence of our true identity. Insecurity leads us to not take responsibility for ourselves; it leads us to fear our own light and prefer our own shadow, which, at least, we are familiar with.

> *Insecurity is responsible for how society moves. Everything is uncertain: your relationship with your partner is insecure, your love is insecure, everything is insecure. You will discover that everything is insecure and in this insecurity you expect to find security. This is the biorhythm of life; but if you discover and find your insecurity, then you will be yourself, because if one finds insecurity within themselves then it means he begins to know who he is.[18]*

We cannot find our own insecurities and confront them unless we deal with situations that make them arise. This will lead us to get to know ourselves and feel secure. We cannot have a new and interesting experience if we remain relegated in our insecurity. Life is a gym where we can train the muscle of awareness to guide our mind toward knowing our true self. Otherwise, how else can we find out our value and our latent potential? How can we explore new states of awareness? How can we wear new mental habits and discover our infinite inner resources if our insecurity makes us avoid the unknown? We can get to know areas of ourselves, of others, and of situations only by relating to them and allowing ourselves to be fully in the experience.

In acting workshops, we used improvisation techniques—sensory exercises in which we would identify with an animal, a tree, or a picture, physically reproducing its posture, facial expression, and body language. I still remember my first experience vividly: A man and a woman decided to represent Michelangelo's masterpiece, the Pietà, improvising in front of us all. The rest of the group was divided into roles—one person was the director, another was the set designer, and another was the costume designer, and everyone cooperated to reproduce this famous work of art depicting the body of Jesus on the lap of his mother Mary after the Crucifixion. We found a chair and sat our Mary, now a successful comic actress, on the stage. As we helped her wear the shawl and veil, the atmosphere in the room was still detached and amused. When the woman's position resembled that of the statue, we helped our Jesus sit on his mother's lap. Slightly clumsy, they struggled to relate to one another in a position that was uncomfortable for both. We all joked and laughed, someone made nervous gestures, someone snorted and cried out to release the tension. Our Jesus, now wearing only a loincloth, had to try to abandon himself helplessly in his mother's arms. After shifting her right foot to support her son's back, holding his head between her armpit and her breast, the woman's face became serious. The actor struggled to let go; he felt insecure and far too heavy for her. Eventually, however, he persuaded his body to surrender. This process of abandonment gave him shivers and shakes. In turn, she began to feel the physical pain of maintaining that position under the weight of his body. We asked them both to continue and accept what was happening to them. The director brought them back in line with the position of the sculpture. She cried out, her right arm hurt, and she suffered trying to keep her son from falling off her lap. The grimace of pain transformed her face; she raised her right shoulder and tilted her head sideways to compensate. Now, for the first time, the posture was almost completely exact. She understood this, before recognizing it through her senses, from the atmosphere in the room, where everyone seemed to have suddenly stopped breathing. Just by reproducing the posture and the interaction, something was happening. But although moving and compelling, it still felt generic, unspecific.

After the first wave of emotions, the two actors intuitively understood the next step: They must play the role from within. He must die like Christ, and she must become the mother of this dying Jesus, serene in the tragedy of losing him physically. She understood this but couldn't experience it until, worn out by the force of gravity, split in half by the weight of her son, her arm holding him up stretched her chest and finally opened her heart. By reflex he stopped controlling his body and completely surrendered to her and to himself. I felt a wave rising from my chest as I saw the effect this representation had on the whole group. It was hard to understand where her sweat ended and where her tears began. He fought between giving up to emotional release or giving in to the liberation of death. His body naked and cold, he burst out when we turned his head toward us and arched his neck. That open neck and face turned toward us gave him truth and consistency. We helped her stretch her right arm behind his back until her fingers spread under his armpit and dorsal muscle. The position of the hand and fingers reset her brain. Her emotions calmed down, as she contemplated what was happening and tried to accept what she was feeling. With some difficulty, we slipped her left hand out from under his legs, and she automatically rotated her palm upward, both a request for help and an acceptance of a greater will. She changed; her neck relaxed, her chin reclined, her face became beautiful and radiant. She lowered her eyelids so that it was not clear whether her eyes were closed or were imbued with the sight of her child.

Together, they were perfect. They were a prayer; they had become Michelangelo's Pietà. From just a photo of a sculpture, they evoked a state of awareness on a specific nuance of the whole range of human potential, influencing the entire group. Each person, in his own way, experienced it.

Slowly we pulled them out of the posture. No one dared speak; we could barely look at each other, make hand contact, hug each other. That is the beauty of a transcendental experience: nothing to add, nothing to remove. I had seen Michelangelo's sculpture for the first time as a child, in St. Peter's Basilica. At the time, I was left fascinated and speechless. But now, I had experienced it, I understood it, I had lived it.

In yoga, our body's physical limitations often pose challenges as we try to hold a posture. We can choose to give up, or we can let go of the need to control, rise to the occasion, and surrender to the posture. In Yogi Bhajan's words:

> *There is one line in Asa di Vaar and it's in the words of Naanak:*
>
> **duyee kudrat saajee-ai kar aasan ditho chaa-o**
>
> *"God sat in a posture to see the graceful happiness of Himself and His Creation."*
>
> *That is the power of the posture! Aasan is not a small thing. Aasan means also "seat." It means elementary power on which you house your consciousness. People don't understand, they think this is all a joke. No! Posture is your foundation on which is a hub—on which all your movement is calculated. If you do not have a deep steady posture—you have nothing![19]*

To excel, we need to let life test us. In this experience, our qualities will surface, and we shall know ourselves. The question is, how do we allow ourselves to be in the intensity of the relationship with ourselves, with others, with an idea, with a commitment? Reflect on the process the two actors went through. Now extend those feelings to the length and breadth of our relationships and dynamics. Are we able to get to the bottom, to remain until the experience is complete—until each resistance has been released, each fear has been overcome, each attraction or repulsion has been dissolved? Can we stay until our being finds an answer, until it finds the qualities and depth necessary to go through the experience and transcend a contracted and limited state to find ourselves in a new and elevated state? Can we show such determination? Can we accept the challenge? Or at each crossroads, will we look for a possible way out to relieve the pressure, shun the challenge, avert the possibility of losing and suffering, thus avoiding the experience of our true self? Take the simplest and most common example: During a bout of flu, a fever, a severe headache, infection, or joint pain, any nonserious ailment, do we ever allow ourselves to listen to our body, give it time to process the disease, and activate its innate ability to heal itself, before taking medicine? How many times, just to cover the symptom or suffer less, did we choose the fast way out—the one that doesn't cure and doesn't resolve the problem but only prevents pain, untraining the body to find its own appropriate immune response? All the body needs is time to heal, but it is never allowed it, because our nervous system is unable to contain what is happening. The two actors in the Pietà went through a wide range of emotions and various states of consciousness in order to grasp that transcendence; in doing so, they healed the deepest levels of their being and quite possibly their family constellations, too.

We don't necessarily have to wait for life to offer us the opportunity, through joys and tragedies, to enrich our levels of feeling, to evoke our abilities, to know ourselves, and to excel. If we did that, time would be a very severe teacher. Kundalini Yoga, through meditations and kriyas, provides us with the technology to make important and precise shifts in awareness. This discipline allows us to experience states of consciousness of which we may only know the name. It does not suggest a strategy or behavior. Rather, it evokes an inner attitude that leads to behaviors, decisions, and communication skills appropriate for dealing with external stimuli, consistent with our own identity. Our awareness shifts, which gives us a fresh perspective that clearly, simply, and effectively makes us see the thing we are relating to. The result is an intervention on the cause of the problem, not on the effect. Kundalini Yoga does not focus on the consequence or on the symptom, but on the cause that has been moved to have this particular effect. This too is the purpose of this book: to provide knowledge and ancient wisdom through examples of current situations, offering simple holistic tools that can enable us to find the state of consciousness from which we can live in the authenticity of ourselves, no matter what we are facing. How much are we willing to experiment, and where do we stop?

You are you, and not someone else. Find out who you are and manifest it, even if this means risking being arrogant. Influence the space and environment around you, without limiting yourself. Inspire others to do the same. If we are here on planet earth, we are here for a purpose. Living for this purpose is the only way we can be free and excellent. In doing so, relax and rejoice.

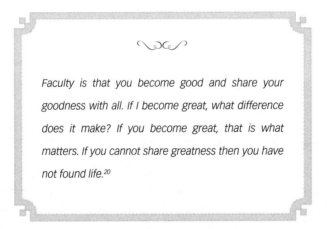

Faculty is that you become good and share your goodness with all. If I become great, what difference does it make? If you become great, that is what matters. If you cannot share greatness then you have not found life.[20]

Elementary Adjustment of the Brain

April 22, 1993

When a human has come into his understanding of his or her own dignity, there is no power on earth which can shake it.

~Yogi Bhajan

The following elementary adjustment will change the third layer of the neurons in a single rhythm and will regulate the first ring under the stem of the brain.

1. Sit in Easy Pose with the spine straight. The thumb touches the Mercury mound at the base of the pinkie finger. The Sun finger (ring) and the Mercury (pinkie) finger bend over the thumb, holding it in place. The Jupiter (forefinger) and Saturn (middle) fingers are straight. Bring the hands in front

of the Heart Center with the palms face down and the Jupiter and Saturn fingers of each hand pointing toward each other. The forearms are parallel to the ground and the elbows are wide.

Make an "O" of your mouth and inhale through the rounded mouth and exhale forcefully through the nose. The force of the exhale will cause the nose to wrinkle.

Keeping the elbows in place, as you exhale through the nose, extend the forearms outward so that the Jupiter and Saturn fingers point forward and the arm creates a 90-degree angle. When you inhale through the mouth, return to the original position. Focus your eyes on the tip of your nose. 3 minutes.

This exercise will cause the back area of the head to vibrate. It will give oxygen directly to your brain, stimulate your pituitary and totally fix the vibrator which is called the pineal. It is effective for relieving loss of memory, loss of feelings, and nightmares.

To end: Inhale deeply, hold your breath for 10 seconds while you lock your back molars and tighten all your muscles. Exhale forcefully with a Cannon Breath through the mouth. Repeat twice more and relax.

2. Sit in Easy Pose with a straight spine. Extend the Jupiter (forefinger) and Saturn (middle) fingers straight while you bend the Mercury (pinkie) and Sun (ring) fingers and lock them down with your thumb. Bend the elbows so that the hands are near shoulder level with the Jupiter and Saturn fingers pointing

straight up. Rotate your arms in small outward circles as fast as you can, while you breathe rapidly through your rounded mouth. The breath is a rapid diaphragm breath through the rounded mouth. There will be a "hoo, hoo, hoo" sound similar to the sound baboons make. The diaphragm will move as fast as a hummingbird's wings. 3 minutes.

To end: Inhale deeply, suspend the breath for 10 seconds; tighten all the muscles and tightly press the lips together. Exhale forcefully, Cannon Breath through the mouth. Repeat this sequence twice more and relax.

3. Keep the hands in the same mudra as Exercise #2. In Easy Pose, extend your arms out to the sides, with the palms facing up and the Juper and Saturn Fingers pointing to each side. Twist the hands backward as far as possible. The inner elbow with stretch toward the back as the hands twist; there will be a healing pain in the elbows. If the elbows are twisted properly, the chest will automatically press forward and the rib cage will lift. Hold this

position and breathe naturally. Correctly done, this posture will cause the serum in the spine to change, bringing a renewed youthfulness and balance to the body. 3 Minutes

To end: Inhale deeply, suspend the breath for 10 seconds, and lock the back molars. Tighten all the muscles and twist the elbows with maximum effort. Exhale forcefully with Cannon Breath through the mouth. Repeat twice more and relax.

Epilogue

Now let's return to the Kriya, Unfold the Values and Deliver Success, and discover how each exercise supports us as we experience Yogi Bhajan's Eight Elements of Excellence:

The First Exercise stimulates the praana to expand, especially from the area of the diaphragm to the brain, bringing clarity and foresight. The boost in venous flow that returns to the heart increases circulation and purifies the blood along with our thoughts. The centrifugal force loosens the scheme of our thought patterns and preconceptions. The illusory veil of Maya falls, or at least lifts just enough to allow a *vision* of the possible future.

In the Second Exercise, the pressure of the fingers on the armpits restores the balance between the sympathetic and parasympathetic nervous systems, in which the praana is equally distributed and further released by the striking of the arms on the ribs, especially the seventh rib. The heart, already open, begins to expand its electromagnetic field, giving a strong sense of wholeness and self-confidence, which in turn gives us *courage*.

In the Third Exercise, the movement of the outstretched arms helps open up all the meridians that expand from our heart center. Breathing from the mouth cools us down and almost relieves the body and mind, strengthening the effects of the previous exercises. The head is empty and open. The heart is full and fearless.

In the Fourth Exercise, the coordination between Breath of Fire and the alternate movement of the legs synchronizes and balances the two cerebral hemispheres. Pumping the navel and lifting the legs stimulates the Third Chakra and gives our courage new endurance, which results in *grit*.

The Fifth Exercise strengthens the work on the Third Chakra. The invisible umbilical cord that continues to draw nourishment from the universe is now perceptible, and gives strength and power, as if God Himself were sitting in our Third Chakra. We stop behaving like victims. We become *humble*, and can no longer be humiliated.

The Sixth Exercise requires the total involvement of every single abdominal muscle in the region of the Third Chakra, the fulcrum of our motor and nervous intelligence is revealed. The experience of the application of creative intelligence in action gives us *knowledge*.

Through the Seventh Exercise, we have now achieved a balance between the nervous and glandular system. The navel and the heart, personality and True Identity are now connected. The consistency between strength and structure, and neutrality and amplitude, creates a space of prayer. The mantra, which sets our deep intention, is a *prayer* in itself.

Eighth Exercise: With the nervous system under pressure, we increase the frequency of our prayer's intention, projecting it out into the future, to the Infinite. As we project the essence of ourselves, the nobility of the posture and the vibration of the mantra evokes in us a state of *grace*.

In the final exercise, the projection receives a response, precise and accurate in space and time. From the Unknown into our hands, hearts and in every cell, we perceive attainment and achievement. Now, thanks to the flow of the kundalini up the spine, we are the connection between heaven and earth. The magnetic field is fully expanded and pregnant with our virtues. Exchanging and receiving from our infinite essence allows us to deliver, with absolute *determination. This is Excellence.*

Endnotes

1. Quote by Yogi Bhajan taken from Gurucharan Singh's *"Kundalini Yoga and Meditation as Quote by Yogi Bhajan from A Contemporary Approach to Human Excellence and the Thirst of the Soul"*.

2. Yogi Bhajan. (2009). *Man to Man: The Men's Teachings of Yogi Bhajan, PhD*. Espanola, NM: Kundalini Research Institute.

3. The instructions for this kriya are from the contemporaneous notes of Guru Rattan Kaur and could not be verified by KRI Review. Originally published as *"For Immunity"* in Guru Rattan Kaur's *Transition to a Heart-Centered World*.

4. Yogi Bhajan. (1994). Break the Mind's Hypnotic Trance. In *Mind and Meditation* (4 DVD Set) from *Mind and Meditation Level 2 Manual, Study Guide 2*. Espanola, NM: Kundalini Research Institute.

5. Yogi Bhajan. (1992). Be Happy, Be Neutral: An Experience with Yogi Bhajan. Mental Intrigues: The Games People Play. *Mind and Meditation Level 2 Manual.* Espanola, NM: Kundalini Research Institute.

6. Yogi Bhajan. (2002). *Kundalini Yoga as Taught by Yogi Bhajan.* Espanola, NM: Kundalini Research Institute.

7. © 1985 *The Teachings of Yogi Bhajan.*

8. Yogi Bhajan. (2001). *The Journey of Consciousness.* Espanola, NM: Kundalini Research Institute.

9. © 2001 *The Teachings of Yogi Bhajan.*

10. From *"Radiance & Victory. A woman's way to prosperity"* by Dr. Manjit Kaur Khalsa and Siri Tapa Kaur Khalsa.

11. Yogi Bhajan. (2005). *The Aquarian Teacher: KRI International Kundalini Yoga Teacher Training Textbook Level One Instructor.* Third Edition. Espanola, NM: Kundalini Research Institute.

12. Yogi Bhajan. (2006). *The Conversation between Your Known & Unknown, Level Two Conscious Communication Manual.* Espanola, NM: Kundalini Research Institute.

13. Ibid.

14. Yogi Bhajan. (1989). Stop Your Mental Games. In *Mind and Meditation: An Experience with Yogi Bhajan* (4 DVD Set) from *Mind and Meditation Level 2 Manual.* Espanola, NM: Kundalini Research Institute.

15. © The Teachings of Yogi Bhajan, October 9, 1990.

16. Yogi Bhajan. (1989). Stop Your Mental Games. In *Mind and Meditation: An Experience with Yogi Bhajan* (4 DVD Set) from *Mind and Meditation Level 2 Manual.* Espanola, NM: Kundalini Research Institute.

17. Atma Singh Khalsa and Guruprem Kaur Khalsa. (2011). Live Above Denial. In *Meditations for the New Millennium.* Espanola, NM.

18. © The Teachings of Yogi Bhajan, April 22, 1993

19. © The Teachings of Yogi Bhajan, September 11, 1990

20. © 1984 The Teachings of Yogi Bhajan.

Index

About the Author

Sadhana Singh, with twenty years experience in stretching and gymnastics, is a Kundalini Yoga Lead Trainer dedicated to serving and empowering new teachers and future trainers. An inspired author and dedicated counselor, he is also responsible for "L&MKYT Leadership & Management Kundalini Yoga Training" and for the "Crystallizing the Diamond" project. The Yoga of Asana, The Yoga of Pranayama, and Pratyahar are part of this project. Sadhana Singh lives in Rome, Italy.

(portrait by Coco Van Oppens)